James Liddy
A Critical Study

ARLEN ACADEMIC

The Austrian Anschluss in History and Literature
Eoin Bourke

James Liddy: A Critical Study
Brian Arkins

A Reader's Guide to Rilke's Sonnets to Orpheus
Timothy J. Casey

Conserving the Emerald Tiger:
The Politics of Environmental Regulation in Ireland
George Taylor

Exploring John's Gospel:
Reading, Interpretation and Knowledge
Colm Luibheid

Nineteenth-Century Ireland Through German Eyes
Eoin Bourke

James Liddy
A Critical Study

Brian Arkins

Arlen House
Galway
2001

First published March 2001

Published by:

Arlen House
PO Box 222
Galway
Ireland

&

42 Grange Abbey Road
Baldoyle
Dublin 13
Ireland

www.arlenhouse.ie

ISBN paperback 1–903631–07–6
ISBN hardback 1–903631–08–4

Cover design: Dunleavy Design, Salthill, Galway
Typesetting: Arlen House
Printed by: ColourBooks, Baldoyle, Dublin 13

CONTENTS

for David and Susan

James Liddy
A Critical Study

INTRODUCTION

James Liddy – A Critical Study is the first book-length study of the poetry and prose of James Liddy, whom John Asbery considers "one of the most original among living Irish poets".

The book's opening chapter establishes a number of personal and literary backgrounds against which Liddy's work can be assessed. The three key personal elements in Liddy's identity are that he is Irish, Catholic, gay:

> I will have to say straightaway that being queer, like being Irish and being Catholic, has charted my imagination.

The crucial literary precursor in Ireland for Liddy is Patrick Kavanagh who educated him in McDaid's pub in Dublin and showed how poems could be made from ordinary experience. Other crucial literary precursors share an antinomian approach to life: Baudelaire, Whitman, Kerouac.

Chapter Two analyses Liddy's poems that deal with the landscape, people, and history of Ireland. The main treatment of landscape is the volume *Corca Bascainn* (1979) that investigates both nature and people in that part of County Clare. For Liddy, the most important Irish person is his mother, who is seen, with great honesty, as the source of his homosexuality. In Liddy's volume *Trees Greener Than Warm* (1991), Parnell's constitutional nationalism is seen as the way for Ireland to become free.

The book's central chapter – "A Faggot Heaven: The Theme of Gay Sex" – analyses Liddy's poems about gay sex that wonderfully mix passion and intellect, obscenity and tenderness. In so doing, these poems present a combination of honesty that involves pain and of celebration that does not rule out fulfilment. Paramount at all times is the concept of sex as a form of energy, as "existing ecstasy material". Of special significance is Liddy's volume *Baudelaire's Bar Flowers* (1975) that makes vividly explicit the implicit sexuality of the French poet ("Je t'aime" becomes "I fuck you like this"), and justifies Liddy's bold claim that "I have the observance of the sexual life".

Chapter Four, "We Need Brevity: Epigrams and Epitaphs", examines Liddy's brief poems in the volume *Art Is Not For Grown-Ups* (1990) and the chapbook *Epitaphery* (1997). Drawing on the Greco-Roman tradition of brief, witty, pared-down epigrams, Liddy debunks various Irish and American pieties as he writes of literature, sex, and religion. For him, "nothing is more pious or required of the Irish artist".

The book's final chapter examines Liddy's novella *Young Men Go Walking*, which describes bohemian life in Dublin in the 1960s in terse, non-hierarchical prose. Amid a flow of endless talk in which nothing happens more than twice, the novella evokes a Dublin of the alienated who seek endless gratification from drink, sex, and idleness. Bohemian *chaos* replaces bourgeois *cosmos*.

An Epilogue analyses the appearance of most of the above mentioned themes in Liddy's latest volume, *Gold Set Dancing*, which appeared in 2000.

CHAPTER ONE

Backgrounds Personal and Literary

1

James Liddy is one of Ireland's leading contemporary poets. Combining Kavanagh's sense of local place with the cosmopolitan allegiances of MacNeice, exhibiting a Joycean sensibility that is Catholic, sexually open, and devoted to the quotidian, Liddy has proceeded to write some of the most original poetry to come out of Ireland since Yeats. He has, in particular, produced a very powerful body of poems about sex, for which there is no Irish analogue.

Liddy's poetic career spans nearly forty years, his first volume *In a Blue Smoke* appearing in 1964. This was followed by *Blue Mountain* (1968), *Baudelaire's Bar Flowers* (1975), *Corca Bascainn* (1979), *At the Grave of Father Sweetman* (1984), *A White Thought in a White Shade* (1987), *Art is Not for Grown Ups* (1990), *In the Slovak Bowling Alley* (1990), and *Trees Warmer than Green* (1991). *Liddy's Collected Poems*, which was published by Creighton University Press in 1994, contains material from all these volumes, as well as a considerable number of new poems – twenty-four – under the rubric *She is Far from the Land: Poems 1989–93*. In 1997 Liddy published a chapbook called *Epitaphery*, and in 2000 a volume entitled *Gold Set Dancing* appeared.

Despite this body of achieved work, Liddy has not received the critical attention he deserves; part of the reason being that he has lived for several decades now in America. This book aims to remedy that situation by providing a comprehensive introduction to Liddy's work. That such a task is eminently worthwhile is confirmed by critics as diverse as John Ashbery and Desmond Egan. Ashbery asserts of Liddy:

> I consider him to be one of the most original among living Irish poets, perhaps the most. His work has not received the attention accorded his more famous contemporaries, Seamus Heaney and Thomas Kinsella, for example, but I am convinced of its superiority.[1]

And Egan writes:

> Liddy's best poems are wonderful. They have a seriousness, a depth, a tragic insight that few Irish poets – and none of the P. R. poets – could match.[2]

II

Irish, Catholic, gay – these are the three key elements in Liddy's identity:

> I will have to say straightaway that being queer, like being Irish and being Catholic, has charted my imagination.[3]

We will begin with the Irish Catholic side.

Liddy was born in 1934 to an Irish father, who was a dispensary doctor in Coolgreany in County Wexford, and an Irish-American mother. Liddy was passionately attached to his mother – as a number of poems, notably "Clare, the Butterflies", make clear – and without equivocation he attributes his homosexuality to her: "Because he loved his mother he loved men" (CP 237).

The Irish Free State that Liddy grew up in was a homogeneous, indeed organic society that was dominated by a cosy cartel of State, church, and middle class; a comfortable, bourgeois world that demanded conformity and had little time for dissent.[4] But Liddy contrived to have the best of both worlds: he was happy to accept Irish nationalism and Catholicism, but he also turned out to be a poet and to be gay. A neat balancing act managed also by Micheál Mac Liammóir.

Liddy was educated by Benedictine monks at Glenstal Abbey in County Limerick, and quotes Rilke to the effect that "a Catholic childhood is a preparation for a mythical state of mind".[5] Such a mental universe readily responds to the concept of God; acknowledges the supernatural aspects of nature; is, through the "cadences of church Latin in the choir at office", finely attuned to the aesthetic.[6]

But for Liddy, Catholicism cannot be the passive acceptance of a culturally constructed moral code. Like Blake, Liddy stresses the antinomian aspect of Christ:

> The relatives of Jesus
> thought he was out of his mind
> (CP 338)

For an Irishman of Liddy's generation, this inevitably means that he cannot endorse an obsession with sexual morality that has no foundation in the Four Gospels and derives from the economics of the small farm in post-Famine Ireland (no sex outside marriage, late marriage for the eldest son who inherits the farm).[7] The origins of such attitudes go back, of course, much further to Augustine and other figures in the Latin tradition, Greeks like Gregory of Nyssa being much more positive about the body:

> the Latins have a garden named Gethsemane
> different from the Greeks
> (CP 358)

For Liddy, Irish nationalism is also central to his identity. The particular brand of nationalism with which he identifies is that of the Irish Parliamentary Party as led by Parnell and

Redmond. This favours Home Rule for Ireland and may be regarded as the ancestor of the present Fine Gael party. Significantly, Liddy was taught at Glenstal by Matthew Dillon, the son of John Dillon, who was the last leader of the Irish Parliamentary Party, and who:

> poured into our ears the consciousness of a Catholic conservative nationalism that was wonderfully informed, but limited in scope.[8]

Liddy points out that "Some of this high-flow, low-key, cultural nationalism has stayed with me".[9] This is most obviously seen in Liddy's constant response to the quotidian reality of Ireland – its landscape, people, drink, but also in the volume *Trees Warmer Than Green* (1991) that deals directly with themes from Irish history and, in particular, with Parnell. Liddy's allegiance to Parnell can be summed up in this statement from a poem about the revolutionary Maud Gonne:

> Yes, a Republic had to be build
> but it should have been trotted to
> slowly, less gaudily

> (CP 280)

III

A further crucial element in Liddy's identity is his homosexuality and his practice of a gay life style for a lot of his adult life in America. Liddy echoes Michael Denneny's statement that "I find my identity as a gay man as basic as any other identity I can lay claim to", when he asserts:

> I will have to say that being queer, like being Irish and being Catholic, has charted my imagination.[10]

Liddy's homosexuality should be placed in a broader modern context – as is done by George Steiner and Susan Sontag.[11] Steiner points out that:

> Judaism and homosexuality (most intensely where
> they overlap, as in a Proust or a Wittgenstein) can be
> seen to have been the two main generators of the
> entire fabric and savor of urban modernity in the
> West.

Sontag concurs and elaborates:

> Jews and homosexuals are the outstanding creative
> minorities in contemporary urban culture. Creative,
> that is, in the truest sense: they are creators of
> sensibilities. The two pioneering forces of modern
> sensibility are Jewish moral seriousness and
> homosexual aesthetics and irony.

And the homosexual life-style of urban America offers the
best opportunity of fulfilment for a gay man; as Anthony
Burgess says, "The best homosexuality is in America, like
the best everything else".[12]

Liddy, then, lives as a gay man in urban America and
writes out of an imagination that is fuelled by that sensibility.
Which has a number of different facets: an aesthetic that
stresses ambiguity and hence irony; a sense of being set
apart;[13] a view of sex as both passionate and ludic.

In a defining assertion, Liddy brings two of these facets
together:

> there are two reasons for
> keeping alive: being in love and ambiguity
>
> (CP 303)

Equally important is the difference between a gay man and
the straight majority:

> the point of being homosexual ... is, I imagine, that you
> are not part of what is generally going on.[14]

This ironic sense of being different is most obviously found
in sex itself, so that Rechy nicely speaks of "the unique,
sensual, feeling, elegant sensibility of the sexual outlaw".[15]
Or, in Liddy's words:

> this black mystery
> Of you and a few others being chosen.

And difference is practised more generally in the adoption of a Bohemian lifestyle:

> If our country is Poetry then the name of the universe is Bohemia[16]

No closet homosexual, Liddy fully acknowledges his gay identity; he presents homosexuality not as a disease or as childish, but as sensual and ludic. Consequently, Liddy rebukes Somerset Maugham who, though loving a man, did not think of himself as gay; and he avoids both the sexual morbidity of T. E. Lawrence and the sentimentality of Forster's *Maurice*.[17] With Liddy, Irish gay art has come of age.[18]

IV

To these personal backgrounds of Liddy – Irish, Catholic, gay – must be added a number of crucial writers and their literary texts. We are not talking here of "influence" or even of "intertextuality", for these terms do not convey what is involved: Liddy, like so many creative artists, *appropriates* what he needs from his predecessors. Indeed as Borges holds, "The fact is that every writer *creates* his own precursors".[19] Liddy's creations are cosmopolitan, ranging from Kavanagh and MacNeice in Ireland, to Ronsard and Baudelaire in France, to Whitman and to Kerouac (and other Beats) in America. A common thread is a commitment to a bohemian world-view.

Drawing on these created precursors, Liddy has produced an impressive aesthetic, the most notable formulation of which is found in the poem "Kerouac's Ronsard Dance" (CP 228–30). Here Liddy explicitly identifies with Ronsard: "Ronsard, c'est moi". Then taking account of Ronsard's great love sequences to Cassandre, Marie, and Hélène; of his celebration of drink in his epitaph for Rabelais; and of his *carpe diem* philosophy in the poem "Quand vous serez bien vieille", Liddy proceeds as poet-priest to tell us what really matters:

> the four first things: Bacchus, Love,
> the Muses, Apollo

These may be glossed as drink, sex, poetry, and the quotidian:

> the fact of waking
> to every day

two of them, sex and poetry, are among the four types of divine madness listed by Plato (*Phaedrus* 265b).

What Liddy's four first things have in common is that they are forms of *energy*, an entity that, unlike the atom, cannot be split. Consequently, they interact: "without sex there could be no music, no poetry" (CP 322). Furthermore, these forms of human energy are endorsed by the Incarnation of Christ:

> I keep having Cana moments
>
> His body holy
> only to those who know what bodies are.

An aesthetic has now become a metaphysic; a metaphysic that has been earned because of its rootedness in quotidian experience and that seeks to overcome facile dualisms. Thus Liddy is simultaneously the poet of the everyday and of what lies behind the everyday.

V

Analysis of Liddy's relationship to other poets must begin with the Irish poets Patrick Kavanagh and Louis MacNeice. Indeed Liddy was born in 1934 a few years before the publication of two major long poems by the founding fathers of post-Yeatsian Irish poetry, *The Great Hunger* by Patrick Kavanagh in 1942 and *Autumn Journal* by Louis MacNeice in 1939. In very different ways, the examples of Kavanagh and of MacNeice are crucial to Liddy's poetry.

Liddy has asserted that he was educated by Benedictine monks at Glenstal and by Patrick Kavanagh in McDaid's pub in the centre of Dublin. The impact of Kavanagh was both immediate and lasting:

> before him I had only read, and read about, poets. Then I met one which is a very dangerous thing to do. It's like winning big at your first race meeting; you're hooked and that's definite. So I sat, for apparently wasted days and years, in the chapel of McDaid's learning the technique of breathing in what it is to be a poet; an exercise as casual as ordering another round for the master … Ordinary existence gathered something when Kavanagh and his coterie sat at the bar or along the wall![20]

So what Kavanagh did for Liddy (as for many others such as Heaney and Egan) was to validate the ordinary experiences of life and to demonstrate that they can be turned into poetry. In this championing of the ordinary, Kavanagh is in the mainstream of the modern, because one of the central thematic developments in the poetry of the twentieth century, which brings it far beyond the awareness of everyday life in Hardy, is that it is willing to appropriate *any and every sort of material*. As Yeats caustically observed:

> Tristram and Iseult were not a more suitable theme than Paddington Railway Station.[21]

So from the integrated world of a parish in Monaghan, Kavanagh is able, in Egan's words, to 'engineer a remarkable intensity that transcends its immediate origins'.[22] An ability inherited by Liddy in his poems of place, his poems about his family, his poems of ordinary middle-class life.

The influence of MacNeice on Liddy is not nearly so obvious and may well be indirect, mediated through continental and American sources. But MacNeice's famous requirements for a poet are certainly met by Liddy:

> I would have a poet able-bodied, fond of talking, a
> reader of the newspapers, capable of pity and
> laughter, informed in economics, appreciative of
> women, involved in personal relationships, actively
> interested in politics, susceptible to physical
> impressions[23]

For to the ordinary world of Kavanagh, Liddy adds a wide range of political, religious, intellectual, and artistic interests, which ensure that his frame of reference is as broad as MacNeice's in *Autumn Journal*.

Liddy is also like MacNeice in his tendency to produce sharp analytic accounts of complex issues. Compare MacNeice's Aristotelian critique of Plato's "Theory of Forms":

> His world of capital initials, of transcendent
> Ideas is too bleak;
> For me there remain to all intents and purposes
> Seven days in the week.[24]

with Liddy's Incarnational critique of those who trot out the cliché that the human body is the temple of the Holy Ghost (CP 225):

> So they became temples – not temples
> of the Holy Ghost, that sick joke told
> by Christians who want to have nothing
> to do with Christ's body ...

VI

The French romantic poet Baudelaire acted as a catalyst that enabled Liddy to move beyond his early work, which he now views as "one of apprenticeship";[25] for the 1975 volume of versions of Baudelaire called *Baudelaire's Bar Flowers* marks an enormous advance in Liddy's poetry. Pace Bloom's theory of "the anxiety of influence" in which the later poet is always looking over his shoulder at his predecessors,

Baudelaire must be seen as a wholly liberating figure for Liddy.[26]

A large part of Baudelaire's liberating appeal for Liddy lies in the radical sexual persona he adopts, a persona that the Irish poet makes much more explicitly sexual. That sexual persona is, in turn, part of a general antinomian and bohemian attitude that jells with Liddy's own anti-bourgeois views. Detailed analysis of many of the poems in *Baudelaire's Bar Flowers* will be found in Chapter Three.

VII

As is fitting for a man who has lived for the best part of thirty years in America, Liddy has appropriated parts of the American literary tradition, two central debts being to Whitman and to Kerouac (and other Beat writers).

As a recorder of quotidian life and of a vision that lies behind his life, Liddy chimes with the democratic emphasis of Whitman and with his concept of bardic vision.[27] Hence Liddy's poem "Cantico" (CP 330) invokes Whitman's assertion:

> Behold, the body includes and is the meaning, the
> main concern, and includes and is the soul

in order to affirm that bodily experience, which (unlike reality) human beings can bear, is itself spiritual:

> Walt Whitman
> existed either yes or no
> in love
> the body what is practical
> what anyone can bear

This democratic vision of Liddy is notably asserted in the prose poem "In the Bowling Alley" (CP 231–32), where this basic activity is termed "genuine", involves people "living", and is, through the image of the pregnant woman who is bowling, linked to the creation of new life. It is through such a union of spirit and flesh that, as Tobin says, "the ordinary is recognized to be extraordinary".[28]

For Liddy, as for Whitman, sex is clearly a central part of that ordinary experience: just as Whitman affirms that "Sex contains all", Liddy equates "sexual purpose" with "everything that is energy". It is, of course, the poet of insight, the highly individual person, that can chronicle that energy, and, since energy is of the body cum spirit, the poet must turn it into the special, but not the transcendent: "into the creative not the sublime" (CP 173).

VIII

The antinomian element in Whitman is much intensified in Beat writers, on whom Liddy has taught a course for a number of years. People like Kerouac and Burroughs were outsiders who produced a critique of the American ethic of acquisition and of work, and substituted a life-style largely based on sex, drugs, alcohol, fast foods and jazz. It is easy to label such a life-style as hedonistic and self-indulgent, but Kerouac (who was educated by the Jesuits) saw it as spiritual: the Beat Generation was "basically a religious generation" and he himself was a "strange solitary crazy Catholic mystic".[29] Indeed Kerouac's poem "Mexico City Blues" has been called "the finest long religious poem of the twentieth century".[30]

Hence in Liddy's poem "Kerouac's Ronsard Dance" (CP 228–30) that lists his "four first things", Kerouac is the presiding antinomian figure who is identified first with Christ, then with Ronsard, and finally with Liddy himself: "Jesus, Ronsard, Jack, I have become". So while Kerouac could say that he wanted to see God's face, he would also distance himself from the pieties of Gerald Nicosia's 1983 biography of himself that contains 767 pages:

> I'm
> on every page. I was afraid of priests.

The poem "Thursdays Are Serious" gives us the essence of what Kerouac means to Liddy; he is the presiding genius of gay meetings in a bar on Thursdays:

> the Thursday scene,
> loss out
> of Kerouac's pockets, law out of Kerouac's
> glass, a midnight love

Coming from a Breton background and describing the Beats as "fallen angels",[31] Kerouac ultimately offers a form of liberation with a religious aspect that qualifies as majestic art form and key to life:

> Jack Kerouac wines and dines us on
> Thursdays in a far far country. It is all
> stacked up, it flies on light wing then on
> another. We are cellared, cellar angels –
> > that is a tall French dance
> > poème à clef.

IX

We can neatly conclude our analysis of Liddy's literary precursors with the historical link between Kavanagh and the Beat Generation, a topic to which Liddy has devoted an essay.[32] On a visit to America, Kavanagh gave a ringing endorsement to the Beat Generation:

> In fact I would say that the only people in America that are alive are men like Jack Kerouac. *On the Road* is an excellent book, one of my favourite books about America since Henry Miller's *The Air-Conditioned Nightmare*, and I like Corso, Ferlinghetti, and Allen Ginsberg very much ...[33]

Corso reciprocated, telling Liddy in 1982 that:

> Paddy was very sharp ... Kavanagh knew he was a poet so he could sit with whom he liked. Oh, he was a good man, a good poet.[34]

Liddy establishes further connections between Kavanagh and the Beat Generation: those "who possessed the leisure for creation and dissent" practiced bohemian life in Dublin and in San Francisco; enjoyed "authentic homelessness"; shared "elements of antinomianism". One element of which is sexual freedom, so that Ginsberg and Kavanagh became the "architects of the victory of love".[35]

The aesthetic that results from these attitudes requires direct encounter with human experience. Hence Kerouac:

> I have to make my choice between all this and the rattling trucks on the American road. I think I'll choose the rattling trucks, where I don't have to explain everything, and where nothing is explained, only real.

Hence Kavanagh's "Write about what's in front of you, write about what's on the table".[36]

Liddy follows that aesthetic in a brilliant exposition of the antinomian for our time.

Notes:

1   John Ashbery, quoted on back cover of Liddy, *A White Thought in a White Shade* (Dublin 1987).

2   Desmond Egan, *Studies* 77 (1988), 107.

3   "From McDaid's to Milwaukee – Brian Arkins Interviews James Liddy", *Studies* 85 (1996), 339.

4   For an analysis of Ireland after 1922 see B. Arkins, *Planet* 103 (Feb–Mar 1994), 48–61.

5   Liddy (note 3), 334.

6   *ibid.*

7   See Arkins (note 4), 50.

8   Liddy (note 3), 334.

9   *ibid.*

10   Quoted by D. Altman, *The Homosexualisation of America and the Americanisation of Homosexuality* (Boston 1982), 73; Liddy (note 3), 339.

11   Quoted by Altman (note 10), 146.

12   Quoted in Altman (note 10), 216.

13   For the homosexual as different see A. Sullivan, *Virtually Normal* (New York 1995), 198–205.

14   Liddy, *Baudelaire's Bar Flowers* (Santa Barbara 1975), 39.

15   Quoted in Altman (note 10), 148.

16   Liddy (note 14), 8; 12.

17   For homosexuality in literature see J. Meyers, *Homosexuality and Literature 1890–1930* (London 1987).

18   For Irish gay and lesbian writing see *Sex, Nation and Dissent in Irish Writing*, (ed.) E. Walshe (Cork 1997).

19 J. L. Borges, *Labyrinths* (New York 1964), 201.

20 Liddy (note 3), 335.

21 W. B. Yeats, *Essays and Introductions* (London 1961), 499.

22 B. Arkins, "Thucydides and Lough Owel: Interview with Desmond Egan", *Etudes Irlandaises* 14, 2 (1989), 119.

23 Louis MacNeice, *Modern Poetry* (London 1938), 198.

24 Louis MacNeice, *Autumn Journal*, section XII.

25 Liddy (note 3), 336; for an assessment of Liddy's early work see K. Skinner, *New Series: Departures* 1 (1996), 52–60.

26 H. Bloom, *The Anxiety of Influence* (Oxford 1975).

27 For Liddy and Whitman see D. Tobin, *North Dakota Quarterly* (Spring 1997), 116–24, to which I am indebted.

28 Tobin (note 27), 117.

29 For Kerouac see G. Nicosia, *Memory Babe* (Berkeley 1994).

30 Michael MacClure, quoted in Nicosia (note 29), 490.

31 Kerouac, quoted in Nicosia (note 29), 194.

32 Liddy in Patrick Kavanagh – *Midland Conference Papers*, (eds) K. R. Collins, J. Liddy, E. Wall (Omaha 1995), 30–36. For a general estimate of Kavanagh see B. Arkins, *ibid.*, 3–18.

33 Kavanagh, quoted in Liddy (note 32), 30.

34 Corso, quoted *ibid.*, 36; cf. CP 354.

35 *ibid.*, 33.

36 Kerouac and Kavanagh, quoted *ibid.*, 35.

CHAPTER TWO

Ireland: Landscape, People, History

1

Though Liddy has lived for several decades in America, perusal of his *Collected Poems* establishes that the matter of Ireland is one of his main themes. Liddy's Ireland encompasses the three central aspects of landscape, people and history that are closely linked together: the landscape exhibits its history and (as is traditional in pastoral poetry) is peopled; people create history, whether personal or national, as they live in the Irish landscape; history is therefore not an abstraction of wars and of dates, but relates to the reality of the natural environment and of those who inhabit that environment.

Liddy's portrayal of Irish landscape, people and history is, first and foremost, concrete. Not for him the extraordinary vagueness of George Russell ("A.E."), whose verses are rightly seen as getting "woollier and woollier" (*CP* 34). Nor yet the fantasy-world of Swinburne, who, in the "vast decadent network" of England, had midnight dreams of "angelic children whose nakedness titillated" (*CP* 37). Because Liddy, in contrast, is a poet who accepts the validity of the material world and who therefore affirms the minute particulars of life. He may not be able to explain the metaphysical status of those particular objects, but the plain fact of the matter is that things like his local mountain exist,

19

as though Aristotle (or Joyce) had just enmattered their Irish essence[1] (*CP* 33):

> Blue mountains are of themselves blue mountains
> And white clouds are of themselves white clouds
> And there is a blue mountain, Crogher Kinsella,
> And around it there are often white clouds.
>
> Whether all things are accurately themselves
> Or modification of each other I do not know,
> But clear mornings from my bathroom window
> I see white clouds and a blue mountain.

II

From at least the 9th century on and to a degree greater than in any other Western country, poetry in Ireland has been notable for its sense of place. This concern with the vivid depiction of landscape or with the moods of nature has continued through Goldsmith in the 18th century to Yeats, Ledwidge, and Kavanagh, and on to present day poets such as Heaney and Egan.[2] But as well as this preoccupation with place, there is among the Irish a marked concern with the *story* of the place, its history, its legends, its inhabitants, whether human or supernatural; what Sheeran designates *genius fabulae*.[3]

Given that Liddy claims to have been educated by Kavanagh and given Kavanagh's great emphasis on one's local place or parish, it is no surprise to find in Liddy a considerable emphasis on place. Indeed Liddy's poems are characteristically set in a specific place and recount a story about that place, so that they exemplify not merely *genius loci*, but also *genius fabulae*. A few of Liddy's poems deal with Dublin (where he was a student at University College and at the King's Inns in the 1950s), but his stress on landscape is found most obviously in the 1977 volume *Corca Bascainn*, which deals with one of his ancestral landscapes in County Clare (*CP* 67–100).

First, then, Dublin. A city where writer and publisher can both be creative: from Anthony Cronin we have poems that produce the world of Dublin –

> Your words scatter on early days of November
> Into oil trucks in gear over Portobello[4]

– while from Liam Miller, founder of the Dolmen Press and publisher of Liddy's first two volumes, we have:

> beautiful pages he made on an
> endless Baggot St. summer
>
> (*CP* 308)

Indeed Dublin is a city that can be magical: "The moon talked to me in Dublin".[5]

The poem "In a Blue Smoke" (*CP* 23–24)[6] exemplifies that magical side of Dublin, as it celebrates the relationship between a girl and a boy from University College, Dublin, who are in love and kiss in Leeson St. (as their ancestors did before them). Not merely is place now transformed – "they travel in a blue smoke which is the magic of four eyes" – not merely does the poet "pray for the endearments of lovers", but the Incarnate Word ensures the lovers' physical contact: "Christ must journey down from Heaven to multiply their touching". As much about lovers as about their place, this poem sees love as the ultimate: "We are blinded by love, that is the way forward".

Dublin is not always so benign. In the first part of the poem "To the Memory of Sylvia Plath: A Personal Note" (*CP* 26), there is a note of sadness in the world of "Parsons bookshop and the dozen bars" ("my sad kingdom"; "the loneliness of the definable"). But then in the evening the poet comes alive after drinking Guinness and seeing children play, so that "a new era of sincerity is beginning". Tangible proof of which is the poet's strong assertion – which aligns himself with the Sylvia Plath of *Ariel* – that "I'll be reckless". A similar balance is maintained in the poem "Patrick Kavanagh's Dublin" (*CP* 25). On the one hand, we have the potential of this Dublin, whose inhabitants proceed through "wide streets" and carry "white flowers"; on the other hand, these inhabitants enjoy lovers who are "unknowing", and their own commitment is restricted to "walking". Which means that Dublin's potential may never become actual.

III

In Liddy's volume *Corca Bascainn* that is devoted to the landscape and seascape of County Clare, theme and style vary considerably. Thematically, *Corca Bascainn* demonstrates both a commitment to place and to those who inhabit that place. As respectively shown by the titles of the first four sections of the volume – "SHORE"; "SAND HILLS"; "BIRDS"; "CLIFFS" – and by the titles of the poems in the final section "LOVE SONGS OF CORCA BASCAINN": "Tell Us, Streaming Lady"; "History"; "Proverbs of Corca Bascainn"; "I. M. George Fitzpatrick"; "The Anglos Have Gone".

Stylistically, Liddy's main mode in *Corca Bascainn* is that of Joyce's interior monologue – as in Stephen Dedalus' musings on Sandymount Strand. Central to that mode is brevity: *Corca Bascainn* comprises 32 pages of poems, but since a lot of space is not used (some 10 pages), the volume comes to only 22 pages. A brevity enhanced by the fact that, in a number of poems, Liddy uses a very short line, which at times includes only one or two words:

> Wonder
> Land of
>   (*CP* 69)

Liddy also employs other styles in *Corca Bascainn*: an analytic mode not unlike that of MacNeice ("The Anglos Have Gone") and a mode of Blakean paradox ("Proverbs of Corca Bascainn").

The special landscape of Corca Bascainn encompasses nature on the one hand and a variety of beings who inhabit it on the other: contemporary human beings; human beings from the past; mythical figures; the supernatural Sídhe. In general, the first two sections – "SHORE"; "SANDHILLS" – concentrate on nature, while the last three sections – "BIRDS"; "CLIFFS"; "LOVE SONGS OF CORCA BASCAINN" – stress people; but from the beginning nature and human interact. Which again shows that Liddy deals with beings who act in the landscape of Corca Bascainn and so provides us with its *story*.

The minutely observed particulars of the opening section "SHORE" suggest, inevitably, Stephen Dedalus' "ineluctable modality of the visible";[7] indeed, since "Idealism has a hole in it" (*CP* 73), they suggest empirical reality. But we are dealing too with "an imagination of the beach" (*CP* 73) and the minute particulars also function as moral metaphor – as nature does in Horace's *Odes*.[8]

So nature in the form of the sea anemone is a paradigm of desirable simplicity ("Complex structure is a disadvantage" – *CP* 71). Hence the algae are assimilated to "boys and girls", and chemical sexual attraction between the male and female of foods is like that of the human young (*CP* 69–70). But the anemone also produces "poisonous fluid", and so mirrors the violent artists and footballers, who set out to achieve "the classless social beauty" (*CP* 72). Compare the predatory life of the cormorant: existing "In savage oceanland of birds" and "By the pollock holes diving", he becomes:

> Eater
> Daily
> of 11/2 lbs of fish
> (*CP* 80–81)

When in *Corca Bascainn* beings, human and supernatural, become prominent, a variety of moods comes into play. The mood most marked in "CLIFFS" is that of loss. While MacDonnell of the cliffs is as concrete as the cormorant with

> His drinking feats
> His hunting hours

he belongs to a past that no longer exists: since him:

> No one has loomed through the haze
> That should be saluted
>
> *(CP* 85)

Equally well, the mistress at "the pollock holes" is separated from her lord in London – "No one to kiss your cheek" – and their house is bereft of music, games, "of wine and Spanish beer" *(CP* 86). So too the clergy of that epoch are no more:

> No cleric singing wondrous Mass with
> angels in beehive oratory
>
> *(CP* 88)

The modern period can be no less bleak. When the poet contemplates the death by suicide of his friend Paddy, metaphysical Plato – for whom this world is an illusion – replaces empirical Aristotle: we live amid "these false shadows"; can make only "a vague estimate" of nature; listen to "a babel of voices" that come from travellers who are "unseen" *(CP* 83–84).

But in the last poem of "CLIFFS" *(CP* 89–90), Liddy's mood becomes buoyant, as he imagines himself, placed above:

> the shit
> given to me on earth,

upon the cliffs that are perceived to be Platonically "real". Now nature is assimilated to early Christianity (itself constant like a Rock, like Christ), a duo that transcends the manifold inadequacies of the human condition:

> I forget the shit
> Leave hunger
> You are the future.
> Say never ending Masses, fishes.
> Put a cowl on me, Brother storm.
> Sing low with me, Sister waves.

The supernatural is more overtly present in *Corca Bascainn* in the section "SANDHILLS" *(CP* 74–76). Liddy is exploiting the fact that in Ireland the layer of pre-Christian spirituality has never been fully extinguished and that the Sídh or fairies inhabit wild coast-lines, but he can also bring personal witness to bear: he has, as a boy, heard the music of the Sídh, a "Violin sound" that adumbrates:

> Perpetual
> After life

and so makes him "immortal" (the music Carolan is reputed to have heard). Presiding over this music as a "Vision master" and over the drink that goes with it is Donn na Duimcle, a kind of Irish Dionysus exercising "powers from beyond the sunset", with whom the poet wishes to mingle. Indeed Donn is "throwing a party tonight" and the poet, as:

> servant of
> Everlasting pleasures
>
> wants to go.

Cousin to Donn is Angus "the sighing Master of Love", who cures the sexual pain of women and of men. Angus therefore acknowledges the physical reality of sex (as Aristotle might), unlike the Christian followers of Patrick who insist on a ludicrously lofty conception of sex that bears no relation to reality:

> Who make love abstract
> Not a passing hard on

This clash between pagan and Christian worldviews is developed in the poem "[Spring tide swept 'em to the hills]", where the exuberance of the pre-Christian world in Corca Bascainn with its devotion to food, drink, and sex contrasts with ersatz "plaster statues" and "electric candles" in a modern Catholic Church. The vital question that arises from this is how pagan light has been replaced by Christian darkness, what the Neoplatonic philosopher Antoninus called "a fabulous formless darkness mastering the loveliness of the world";[9] for anarchic though the pagan cult of body may seem, it operates within its own type of *kosmos*, order. (And the answer: because institutionalised Churches have a mania for controlling peoples' life-styles).

The section entitled "LOVE SONGS OF CORCA BASCAINN" contains five poems that deal, in different ways, with the inhabitants of Corca Bascainn: they tell of (in sequence) a poem by a man from the area, Comyn; Liddy himself; Blake and Swift as presences in the area; a local Irish resident; and the Anglo-Irish who lived there.

Devoted to the love between the mythological figures of Niamh and Oisin, the poem "Tell Us, Streaming Lady" (*CP* 91–93) comes from the Gaelic poem *Laoi Oisín ar Thír na nÓg* by Michael Comyn who came from near Miltown Malbay and who himself abducted a woman called Harriet Stackpoole. What Liddy stresses here is the validity of sexual desire, as recounted by the two lovers and by Oisín's father Fionn. Such desire is Gaelic and pre-Christian, and was to be vigorously suppressed by the Catholic Free State that came into existence in 1922: "The parts of the body are not in the Gaelic Dev spoke through a shroud" (*CP* 97).

The history that is in question in the poem "History" (*CP* 94–95) is that of Liddy's own career: what are the sources of his poetic inspiration in regard to the theme of love? These prove to be women from Corca Bascainn who, like Diotima of Mantinea in Plato's *Symposium*, are experts on the topic of love. These "girls from Mantinea" first suggest that poetry is written out of deep personal pain, so that the poet must "Follow your lover to the loveless". But they go on to say that such spiritual experience can be replaced with experience that is bodily and godlike: "You'll have to face the hard kiss of a divinity".

In the poem "Proverbs of Corca Bascainn" (*CP* 96–97), the prevailing presence is that of Blake, whom Yeats held to be Irish[10] and who would then:

> have been bard of this
> limestate, these seagulls.

A secondary presence is that of Swift, whom Yeats held to be "always just round the next corner"[11] and who visited Clare, so that "Among the seaweed the Dean is hiding somewhere". Swift finds Clare to be different: there is "no priest", but rather "strange gods", and the place possesses a certain natural inevitability:

> At the end of the road there
> is a shed and night.

The powerful duo of Blake and Swift provide us with a series of paradoxical aphorisms. One approach is to demolish bourgeois platitudes: "If you go out foreign drink the wine not the water"; "The family that pays taxes together stays together". Another approach is to deride the pieties of Irish politics as exemplified in De Valera:

> He looked into his heart to see what Corca Bascainn
> wanted and it turned into stone

But the most striking approach is that of revising Blake. Blake's assertion that "Eternity is in love with the productions of time" turns into "Christianity is in love with the performance of sins", and Blake's "The road of excess leads to the palace of wisdom" becomes "The road of sex leads to the brothel of wisdom". Finally, Liddy's assertion that "The phallic has no opposite" stresses heavily the message: male sexual excess is an essential part of life.

In the poem "I. M. George Fitzpatrick" (*CP* 98–99), a local resident of Corca Bascainn is chronicled. He is a quintessential man of the body and hence advocate of "(The Comic Twilight)". We see him eating a "Jam sandwich"; praising matter in the slope of bog cotton ("Jesus, man, it was lovely"); placed in the context of life-giving water that Thales saw as the source of everything; and asserting that:

> A good piss raises an Irish-
> man's heart
> (*CP* 96)

Consequently, this man's relationship to the body is a guarantee of his worth as a person:

> George Fitzpatrick was a great teacher even if you only
> saw him buying a loaf of bread
> (*CP* 97)

And the appearance at the end of the poem of the curlew, a long-legged wading bird, whose name in French suggests "messenger", indicates that George was a phallic messenger.

The final category of people to be considered in Corca Bascainn are the Anglo-Irish. The title of this last poem in the sequence – "The Anglos Have Gone" (*CP* 100) – simultaneously removes their claims to be Irish and asserts that their day is over; they are to be replaced by the new bourgeoisie of the Free State, by grocers and Catholic clerics. In a significant link, which recalls Yeats's concern for the Big House as well as its occupants,[12] the departure of the Anglo-Irish involves the destruction of the material civilisation they created:

> The verandahs of Moore's and The West
> End are demolished

Symbol of the departed Anglo-Irish is the novelist Charles Lever, who not only worked with victims of a cholera epidemic in County Clare, but also in his later novels deals with the marginalised and was himself buried in Trieste. Liddy's visit in the autumn to this man's grave prompts the poem's final question – "Will there be another Spring?" – that hovers, as we think of Elizabeth Bowen's novel *The Last September*, between being a genuinely open question and being a rhetorical question expecting the answer "no".

IV

Several of Liddy's poems about Irish people deal with his own family, and with people who lived in or near his native place of Coolgreany near Gorey in County Wexford in the South-East of Ireland. Dublin and various American cities are accorded their due, but the native place remains significant as *fons et origo*, as both ordinary and special. A fitting approach from the disciple of Kavanagh, who held that the parochial is crucial;[13]

Parochialism and provincialism are opposites. The provincial has no mind of his own; he does not trust what his eyes will see until he has learned what the metropolis – towards which his eyes are turned – has to say on the subject ... the parochial mentality on the other hand is never in doubt about the social and artistic validity of his parish. All great civilisations are based on parochialism.

Obviously, then, the appropriate poem to begin with here is "Coolgreany" (*CP* 35–36). Liddy provides both a list of quotidian items that includes landscape – "a row of pruned apple trees" – and neighbours – "a ninety year old cobbler still at his last" – and also a special moment: "Maud Gonne riding out on a white horse from Arklow". But what puts Liddy's signature (*sphragis*) on the poem is the inclusion of his own family, father, mother, son:

> The Dispensary House –
> Virginia creeper – the doctor's beautiful wife drinking
> inside – the doctor's son kissing someone –

That kissing of another male at the end of "Coolgreany" adumbrates Liddy's *differentia*, the vocation to be a poet of male love that is referred to in the early poem "A Personal Odyssey" (*CP* 29–30). The first step in such an odyssey is to achieve (in Jung's term) individuation:

> to make myself an individual however peculiar
> I might look or however far I might have to travel ...

The epiphany that then comes for this special person guarantees that love – which is linked to the divine – becomes the central experience of life; must be shared with other men; and is somehow connected with poetry. A prophetic account of how Liddy's life and poetry were to develop.

Liddy's mother Clare, who was so important to him, features in a number of poems, the single most striking account of her being found in the wonderful prose poem "Clare, the Butterflies" (*CP* 203–13).[14] Liddy's style here is exquisite and clearly meets the requirements of Baudelaire (himself no mean exponent of the prose poem):[15]

> Which of us has not dreamt, in his days of ambition, of
> a poetic prose, musical without rhythm and without
> rhyme, pliant enough and jerky enough to adapt itself to
> the lyric movements of the soul, to the undulations of
> dreams, to leaps of perception.

Such a flexible style is matched by flexibility in theme: "Clare" is simultaneously an Irish county, an Irish island, and the Christian name of Liddy's mother; butterflies are both very earthy ("a yellow and white one on Sutton Street in San Francisco") and also metaphysical ("Her soul, this time"). In a clever passage that mixes empathy with hard analysis, mother is special, but by no means perfect:[16]

> She has taste (rare), style (not so rare but most people
> immune to it), flair (flexible in a quarter of the human
> race), poise (pupils of Sacred Heart convents get this),
> elegance (which nobody should have – pulling aesthetic
> rank), class (in both senses, fair and unfair), beauty
> (who deserves this hard beach gift, gritty out of the sea),
> and directness (speaking what you think – an
> intermittent tyranny). Not virtue – plagued. Flip the
> goddess coin. States of mind, she never had: insight,
> self-analysis, temperateness, Celtic imagination,
> peacableness, Christianity (apart from Irish cold rain
> Catholicism), Irishness (apart from Republicanism).

Liddy picks out for mention special moments in his mother's life: drinking Scotch in the Shelbourne, swimming in Potsdam, meeting the President of the Executive Council, enthusiasm for "a hotel near the Opera and Cafe de la Paix" in Paris. What informs all this is a potent combination of the woman's passion for life and of the essential transience of that passion. As Liddy lists with rare poignancy what she will "never again" do, his theme is the Horatian one of the passing of time and of the inevitability of death.

What has been lost with that passing of time is captured in one of Liddy's most relaxed poems "Woodenbridge Golf Club" (*CP* 46–47), in which playing golf with his mother is evoked with pleasing nostalgia:

I remember when golf
was Vespers evening prayer,
light failed behind

Tree on the Avoca River
the fish swam past boulders
for our supper,
I and my mother

in slacks were rapt
putting on the last green
what well being
the world was a cosy womb

When the mist came down
from the valley hillocks
the fairies played golf
elfin and very smart.

A very different mood is found in the poem "Josie" (*CP*
165–66), devoted to the long-serving maid of the Liddy
family. This poem is at once one of Liddy's most emphatic
assertions that daily experience is vital – Josie was person
"whose festivals were many" – and his version of Yeats's
knowledge that:

> where all are in God's eye,
> There cannot be ...
> A single soul that lacks a sweet crystalline cry[17]

For as Liddy's register of language enacts, the donkey, on
which Christ traditionally rode into Jerusalem, paves the way
to God and his gifts:

> Come forward to that donkey path
> of childhood. Reader, do not despise
> because it is small because it is
>
> little. The Lord does everything
> in a mystery, a baptism and a chrism
> and a eucharist and a redemption and a
> bridal chamber.

Further forms of energy are provided by the O'Rafferty
brothers of "My Neighbours Two Brothers" (*CP* 161–64).

John is devoted to backing horses, – horseracing is an activity described by Kavanagh as Dionysiac[18] – so that he spends:

> all day Saturday sleeping
> between races at the counter.

What Ger calls to mind is sexuality, especially the love songs of the Irish and the Troubadours:

> Ger, with your Gaelic libido
> you want to sing a song of Normandy –
> Provence.

A final form of energy is the music dealt with in the poem "Attention: First Lady of the Festival" (*CP* 295–97). As the poem describes the heady atmosphere during the renowned Wexford Opera Festival – drink, tobacco, talk, music that is summed up as:

> a
> pool of Gordon's gin party light

it focuses on Eva Cousins who:

> orbits
> sweetly weakly each Hallow Fest with the pound of Music
> in Wexford streets

Moving beyond the trivia, the energy of her piano-playing chimes with human grief, and yet that energy must, like all else, pass:

> when she
> laid her white bark against the ivories she touched our
> pain with her strife. Her fragments ring together;
> her melody away as China, Chinese airs now, ornamental
> shade tree. She is far from the land.

V

Liddy's central engagement with Irish politics is found in the 1991 volume *Trees Warmer than Green*, the poems in which are (with two exceptions)[19] reprinted in *Collected Poems*. The sub-title of the volume – Notes Towards a Video of Avondale House – establishes that the theme is Parnell and his native place in Wicklow; that a definitive account is not being provided; that the necessary condensation of a visual medium is being observed in 26 pages (compare the recent television series on Parnell).

Parnell dominated Irish (and British) politics for ten years (1879–89); he was perceived to possess an enigmatic personality that combined passion and indifference ("equivocal by nature");[20] and he was ruined because of his sexual relationship with Kitty O'Shea. Such a man inevitably belongs to mythology.[21]

In popular mythology, Parnell becomes the Uncrowned King of Ireland, the Chief, the Blackbird of Avondale – as Liddy's poems attest. In literary mythology, Parnell's fate lies behind Joyce's short story "Ivy Day in the Committee Room", and the famous dispute about his affair with Kitty over Christmas dinner in the *Portrait*. The process of mythologisation reaches dizzy heights in Yeats's late poem "Parnell's Funeral": Parnell has now become a god like Dionysus who dies and rises again. And for Liddy, Parnell has added personal attractions: he came from the neighbouring county of Wicklow and also has a half-American descent.

A Greek analogue for Parnell might be (*mutatis mutandis*) the Athenian politician Alcibiades, who, during the Peleponnesian War (431–04 B.C.), fought first for Athens which rejected him, than for Sparta, then for Athens again, before being murdered through Spartan intrigue. Like Parnell, Alcibiades is the superior aristocrat who:

> refused to learn the flute because he thought it ill became a gentleman either to put his cheeks out of shape or to make music he could not speak to[22]

At the same time, Yeats's Saint singles out "that great rogue Alcibiades" as a specially dissolute person – as Parnell appeared to be to many political and religious leaders after

Kitty O'Shea. But Yeats's ugly Hunchback, in whom every possibility is latent, offers his gratitude most to Alcibiades – as Liddy does to Parnell.[23] For if the State raises such a lion's whelp, it "must accept its ways".[24] After all, even Socrates was attracted to Alcibiades because, as Liddy says:

> the wise in the end will
> often take up with the beautiful[25]

The first two poems of *Trees Warmer Than Grass*, which are addressed to "liberal magistrates" at the time of 1798 rebellion in Ireland – "probably the most concentrated episode of violence in Irish history"[26] – provide historical background for Liddy's poems about Parnell. These poems – "Bicentennial Words for the Liberal Magistrates of 1798" and "To the Liberal Magistrates" (*CP* 266–70) – may be classed as "revisionist" in the sense that they seek to remove popular misconceptions about what happened in 1798. So Coolgreany was "a Protestant village" and Perry's cell of the United Irishmen "had more Protestants than Catholics", two groups who met "on Christmas Eve at least".

These eighteenth-century Protestant magistrates are accorded, à la Yeats, a certain *sprezzatura*: espousing liberal politics, they are devoted to their estates and to horses, to duels and drink. In such a situation, change cannot come from "the handle of a pike" (the Irish version of Mao's "barrel of a gun"), but rather from Parnell's democratic activity:

> Love grows
> from a rose in a Parliament yard

Consequently, Yeats's epitaph[27] must be revised for the liberal magistrates: they are not to look coldly on the human condition, but need to be fuelled by alcohol, and they are not to pass by because they will be reincarnated, but to carry on inexorably with political action because there is no other way:

> Cast a hot hungry eye on the glass, horsemen
> trek on.

Opposed to the restrained nationalism of Parnell is the irredentist and violent nationalism of Maud Gonne (*CP* 278–85). Yeats waxes eloquent about her fanatical quest for Irish freedom:[28]

> Have I not seen the loveliest woman born
> Out of the mouth of Plenty's horn,
> Because of her opinionated mind
> Barter that horn and every good
> By quiet natures understood
> For an old bellows full of angry wind?

Liddy concurs. Maud Gonne is a person who "adores sloganeers" and the white horse (on which she arrives in Coolgreany) becomes a symbol of inflexible attitudes, which her son Sean is asked to abandon. And yet the matter is not so simple:

> Nobody can say
> where victory lies

Because irredentist nationalism can only flourish when genuine grievances exist: the Famine, which for the Irish could involve:

> only an exercise
> in the revolution

and evictions, when:

> today the landlord hunts his tenants from the village
> to the mountain

Indeed from 1879 to 1883, 14,600 tenants were evicted.[29] In the final analysis, then, the way Ireland becomes free is through Parnell's constitutional nationalism:

> Yes, a Republic had to be built
> but it should have been trotted to
> slowly, less gaudily. Who qualifies
> on a white horse?

Liddy's engagement with Parnell is not always conducted in terms of politics: due space is granted to landscape, love, money, drink, and food.

In the landscape of Avondale, the unusual trees – which are "warmer than green" – become a symbol of the enigmatic Parnell and his complex brand of nationalism. For when the Irish people fail:

> to stand under the
> trees

they reject Parnell. The result is that, because of public obsession with Parnell's affair, the private grounds of Avondale are turned into vulgar spectacle:

> A version of the gaze that
> decenters the sexual myth into a
> public park.

The effects of Parnell's illicit affair were indeed devastating. Parnell had to mortgage Avondale "to the hilt"; Kitty "was never seen in Avondale"; was condemned by the Church ("St. Patrick would never have invited Kitty O'Shea to dinner"); and, because of what was arguably a mid-life crisis, Parnell "died from love". All of which suggests that "Being in love means you never get into the clover" (*CP* 276; 273).

Liddy's response to the tragedy of Parnell is to follow Yeats in advocating drink because "Parnell loved a lass".[30] When St. Patrick rejects Kitty on Ivy Day, Liddy asserts that "I'll have to have a few extra rums and cokes" (*CP* 273). Equally well, the King, like everyone else, must eat: for dinner there is grilled trout that "sleeks on the table" (*CP* 272).

Parnell's legacy – which is considerable – exemplifies the way in which the human condition is irrevocably dual.

Parnell can be seen as the focus of positive energy, as the bringer of light and "love that made trees and hotel rooms warm". More: the fact that he could temper this energy with scorn (which was so much greater than that of Yeats) ensured that his achievement "lit Paris" in the shape of Proust who lived there and of Kerouac who visited (*CP* 277).[31] But very great loss cannot be denied either. We have to reckon with the "Chief gone" the way of all flesh, of boats, factories, coastguard stations. We have to reckon with the fact that all those who once knew him and those who knew such people are dead or about to be dead; as the old woman who met somebody who

> had shaken the hand of Mr. Parnell
> in his quarry in the Rock

will soon be dead (*CP* 275).

Then becoming a mythological figure involves being exposed to what Auden calls "unfamiliar affections!"[32] So in the case of Parnell, it is not merely the fact that Avondale House is a tourist attraction, with its "entrance got fit for a viceregal visit", but a local bar is (inevitably) called "Kitty O'Shea's". There is an element of kitsch about this, as Parnell's Helen becomes commercialised instead of burning Troy:

> The face that launched a thousand chivalries will lunch
> A thousand pubs
> > (*CP* 274)

But Liddy cannot be exempt from all this, will himself drink in the Kitty O'Shea lounge in the Hilton in Chicago. And since Parnell sings "not for tourists", but "only for the State" – that is, the people of Ireland – Liddy can, in the final analysis, say "Cheers, Chief". Which is all the more appropriate because Liddy assimilates himself to Parnell – as well as to Joyce – in the poem "June 16, 1982": just as Joyce wrote of Parnell, so too on Bloomsday in Paris does Liddy. Matching the Blackbird of Avondale, Liddy becomes "this little blackbird", an Irish nationalist, but one with a bohemian slant:

> Blackbird of the Left Bank,
> sure I can ruffle my
> green feathers too

Once more Parnell has "lit Paris".

Finally, the poem "Little Song for Ivy Day, 1991" (*CP* 288). Yet again what makes Ivy Day is drink in "bright glasses", as someone sings the original version of "The Dawning of the Day". As alcohol and song celebrate the soul of Parnell, which is "like a burning drill", Liddy envisages the Blackbird of Avondale himself singing to transform the world into a better place of achieved constitutional nationalism:

> If I were the Blackbird of Avondale I would
> Sing down the river of Aungier Street dreams
> the grey-white stones of the house would flow
> on the water, the trees warmer than green.

Notes

1 Cf. R. Ellmann, *Ulysses on the Liffey* (London 1984), 9 on the *Telemachus* episode of Joyce's *Ulysses*: "Every object is clearly defined as if Adam had just given it a name or as if Aristotle had just enmattered its essence".

2 For landscape in Egan (that of the Midlands and Athlone town) see B. Arkins, *Desmond Egan – A Critical Study* (Little Rock 1992), 27–37.

3 P. Sheeran, "Genius Fabulae: The Irish sense of place", *Irish University Review* 18(1988), 191–206.

4 James Liddy, *Blue Mountain* (Dublin 1968), 25.

5 James Liddy, "To Herbert Kubby for his Photograph of me at a Grave in Zurich", back cover, *The Blue Canary* 7 (1997).

6 For this poem see K. Skinner, *New Series: Departures* 1 (1996), 53–54.

7 Joyce, beginning of the *Proteus* episode of *Ulysses*.

8 For this process in Horace see S. Commager, *The Odes of Horace* (New Haven/London 1962), 235–306.

9 Eunapius, *Lives of the Philosophers and Sophists* 471 b. Cf. W.B. Yeats, "Two Songs From a Play".

10 Blake is an important precursor of Yeats, who edited his poems (with Edwin Ellis); see, e.g. H. Bloom, *Yeats* (Oxford 1970), 64–82.

11 W. B. Yeats, *Explorations* (London 1962), 344–45.

12 As in the poems "Coole Park, 1929" and "Coole and Ballylee, 1931".

13 Patrick Kavanagh, *Collected Pruse* (London 1967), 282.

14   A somewhat different version of "Clare, the Butterflies" is found in James Liddy, *A White Thought in a White Shade* (Dublin 1987), 98–101.

15   Baudelaire, *Le Spleen de Paris*.

16   Liddy (note 14), 96.

17   W. B. Yeats, "Paudeen".

18   Cf. Kavanagh, quoted in A. Cronin, *Dead as Doornails* (Dublin 1980), 88: horseracing is "a Dionysiac activity – Apollo has nothing to do with it".

19   "George Moore and the Mermaid at the Meeting of the Waters"; "The First Photograph of the Milesians".

20   R. F. Foster, *Modern Ireland 1600–1972* (London 1989), 401.

21   Cf. Foster (note 20), 426: "The Parnellite era achieved epic status; it was mythologized into "history" as early as *The Times* commission", i.e. 1888.

22   *The Letters of W.B. Yeats*, ed. A. Wade (London 1954), 490–91.

23   W.B. Yeats, "The Saint and the Hunchback".

24   Aeschylus on Alcibiades in Aristophanes' play *The Frogs*.

25   Liddy (note 4), 30.

26   Foster (note 20), 280.

27   W. B. Yeats, "Under Ben Bulben".

28   W. B. Yeats, "A Prayer for My Daughter".

29   Foster (note 20), 408.

30   W. B. Yeats, "Come, Gather Round me, Parnellites".

31   For Kerouac in Paris see G. Nicosia, *Memory Babe* (Berkeley 1994), 547–48.

32   W. H. Auden, "In Memory of W.B. Yeats".

CHAPTER THREE

A Faggot Heaven:
The Theme of Gay Sex

1

Because of what Adrienne Rich has famously called "compulsory heterosexuality",[1] there is a special onus on critics to address gay and lesbian literature; as Alan Sinfield has said, "Ask not what we can do for Englit, but whether it can do anything for lesbian and gay people".[2] Which is simply to recognise the contribution gay people make to literature: "It's true I don't want to join the army", wrote Ginsberg, but "America I'm putting my queer shoulder to the wheel".[3]

Liddy's assertion that "being queer ... has charted my imagination"[4] clearly applies to his art: he has written an important body of poems that deal with homosexual experience, most notably in the volume *Baudelaire's Bar Flowers*. The mood of the homosexual poems captures what Jung called the ambivalence of the archetypes: they enact a combination of honesty, which involves pain, and celebration, which does not rule out fulfilment. In the chronicling of that complex mood, Liddy's precise mixture of passion and intellect, of obscenity and tenderness, has no analogue in Irish poetry, the nearest thing to it being the Crazy Jane poems of Yeats and some Gaelic poetry such as Merriman's *The Midnight Court*.

Indeed Liddy's sexual poems will ensure that he dines at journey's end with Donne: a poet who:

> could be as metaphysical as he pleased, and yet never seemed inhuman or hysterical as Shelley often does, because he could be as physical as he pleased[5]

Part of Liddy's physicality lies in his obscenity and we again need Yeats on Donne:

> His obscenity – the rock and loam of his Eden – but made me the more certain that one who is but a man like us has seen God[6]

All of which justifies Liddy's bold claim that "I have the observance of the sexual life" (CP155).

Sex for Liddy (as for so many others in the contemporary world) is linked to the idea of liberation: "free love free verse free luncheons" (CP186). Another poem provides the necessary explanation of "free love": "Limitless changing unexplored sex".[7] The sex Liddy has in mind is, of course, physical sex between men:

> To make love beautiful
> fucking A, man[8]

The ambiguous syntax of this remarkable epigram permits several meanings: the ludicrous expression "to make love" is definitively glossed by the basic verb "fucking"; the activity of "fucking" transforms "love", so that it becomes "beautiful"; and the capital letter "A" implies not just any man, but a particular one, whose initial that is. Contrary to Platonic definitions of Beauty, here fucking a particular man is beautiful.

Using the figures of Orpheus and of Narcissus, Liddy places this homosexual love in a broader mythical context. Since the poem "Saint Orpheus" is given a special, separate position at the very beginning of *A White Thought in a White Shade* (CP 139–40) and since it is italicised throughout, it is clearly programmatic: Orpheus is the homosexual artist and hence analogue for Liddy. As the myth centrally requires, Orpheus is the archetypal singer whose music affects even "wild beasts". Since he abandoned women for boys after the death of Eurydice, Orpheus is also the patron saint of gay men, whose love avoids "the cares connected with generation". So while Persephone presides over new vegetable life in the Spring and semen goes to produce children, what the homosexual poet creates is amazing art that is from the depths, mad, religious, immortal:

> what the catacombs say is a song,
> immortality, that poetry;
> pure daft, Gospel page-dark.

The myth of Narcissus, on the other hand, deals with what Freud saw as a problem for a homosexual man: narcissism or falling in love with his own image.[9] Liddy sees Oscar Wilde – who, like Narcissus, wasted away until he died – as such a man, a "barker at the Narcissus stall" (CP197). Another example is found amid the drinkers in a gay bar in the poem "Narcissus and the Young Men" (CP323): an older man, identified with Narcissus, ignores a number of young men, who must live in hope that, when the bar closes, he may kiss them.

II

Classic psychoanalytical theory points out that the homosexual man often has a very close relationship with his mother (and an unsatisfactory one with his father).[10] This relationship goes beyond the Oedipus complex – Liddy labels a man "One Oedipal, internal conflict" (CP 222) – and produces an even more intense involvement with the mother. Identifying with the mother, the homosexual man loves men – as she does.

Liddy is completely open about his love for his mother Clare, who, through her appearance in the first and last poems of his *Collected Poems*, becomes his alpha and omega. In a recent interview, Liddy says:

> My mother and I were everything. Princess and
> subject, muse and artist, mistress and servant,
> matriarch and rebel, each possible combination
> except audience and poet[11]

Liddy is even more explicit in poems: "I made my mother
my lover", and:

> Because I loved mother I loved men
> Because I loved mother I loved
>
> (CP 329; 237)

Here Liddy puts a positive gloss on psychoanalytic theory by
attributing his capacity to love to his mother.

A remarkable passage in the poem "How Mother Came
Home"[12] – which deals with the five-year-old Liddy meeting
his parents off the liner from America in Cobh in 1939 –
describes his passion for his mother, implies that his
homosexuality relates to her, and notes that he will therefore
be different, set apart:

> Then they waved and came down
> the gangway smiling and one held out
> the love that fucks the heart day in day out
> and that with passion winds raves the mind.
> She gave me a blue cellophaned basket of
> fruit from New York and a pale yellow
> bunny (my first friend Billy).
> The Goddess pure and in fur coat stole
> the psychic places growing girls should find
> (my emotions will never now be trite).
> Beauty is strange as a secret woody mole.
> From that day forth Mother has been bright.

Much of the long poem "Epithalamion" (CP167–78),
which purports to be about the wedding of Liddy's parents,
deals with *his own* sexual life. Instead of the normal analysis
in an epithalamion of the marriage of a man and a woman,
and of their sexual life, we learn of Liddy's homosexual
lifestyle and infer that this relates to his mother.

Who is indeed lauded in section IV of "Epithalamion".
The initial quotation about Aurunculeia from Catullus' first
epithalamion (61) not only suggests that mother is of

imposing height and from an affluent background, but also (because of the preceding lines) the most beautiful woman in the world.[13] Indeed mother is the Greek goddess Iris, who is, as Liddy says:

> messenger of the gods to me and personification
> of the rainbow

doubtless she will be the "rainbow to the storms of life".[14] From such a goddess and an ordinary Irishman, Liddy was conceived: "The Croppy boy Iris I was".

But in the opening sections (1 and 11) of "Epithalemion", Liddy has already described homosexual experience in a river setting that suggests both section 11 of Whitman's "Song of Myself" and Hopkins' unfinished "Epithalamion" for his brother's wedding. For Liddy, the water of the Inch river is not sanctified like "the generated soul" of Yeats or like the "Spousal love" belatedly adduced by Hopkins;[15] rather, this water is fully sexual and sings "The racking songs of sense love". So in section II of Liddy's poem, Whitman, "The dream bard" who said he was "raided by a perfect mother",[16] is seen as his precursor in writing poetry about young men.

Also relevant is Hopkins' latent homosexuality,[17] which is suggested not only by the depiction of male beauty in his "Epithalamion", and by his assertion that Whitman's mind is "more like my own than any other man's living"[18] but also by the pastoral setting that recalls Theocritus. For Hopkins' extraordinary praise of two poems by Theocritus with a homosexual theme – read Theocritus' *Thalusia* and *Hylas* and Moschus' *Elegy for Bion*, and say if there is anything so lovely in the classics[19] – establishes that he conforms to the general rule in later Victorian literature that mention of Theocritus by a male implies that the man is homosexual.[20] So the latent homosexuality of Hopkins' poem provides a structural model for Liddy, allows him to label Hopkins "a fairy poet" in section I and explicitly invokes Hopkins as homosexual paradigm:

Do I believe Fr. Hopkins was a good – nay an
excellent – fairy poet?
I do, I was there, I read the poem. I lay with a Fairy
by this river,
in Floppy clover

...

I swim, I laugh, I look about,
I watch your freckles curve, I lavish and place my lips
and march down your back.

In section II, by the river near Liddy's school there is
more homosexual activity – "I place my arms round
nakedness" – that recalls Byron's reference to "as many
kisses as would have sufficed for a boarding school".[21] This
form of idyllic sex contrasts with the banality of
conventional marriage, which is ambivalent about sexual
union, opposed to art, restrictive by nature (section 111):
"veil vision is darker than tunnel vision ever was".

Since Liddy's poems so vividly celbrate homosexual
activity and since they assert that this derives from his
mother, it is ironic that what divided mother and son was the
topic of sex:

I saw the open sexual life as an embodiment of love
and purpose, she traditionally saw it as salacious and
rank. She defended monogamy, I adored (sometimes
in moderation) the sybarite[22]

This polarity lies behind the poem "Dear Anima, Show
These Words" (CP 154–55), which occurs at the moment of
his mother's death, placed at Kilkee in County Clare. Liddy
unites religion and sex by urging his mother to believe in:

immortal bliss of saved souls just after sexual
life

but goes on to envisage her soul swimming into ocean
purgation, while he proceeds with life conceived of as a
sensual adventure:

And Mother, inside the house as I sit
on the seawall. You are a star, a cloud,
a hush hush wreath of moonlit water
and you must swim down there
away from the dark rocks to Purgatory.
I have the observance of the sexual life.

III

Liddy has written a number of homosexual poems about particular men: "Love is a Good Read in Bed"; "You came by on bamboo stilts, playing horse ..."; "For Jimin in Manchuria II"; five poems named "Cantico"; "Richard, Oremus".

The poem "Love is a Good Read in Bed" (*WT* 19–20), which describes the poet in bed with a younger man (David Brannan), enacts Liddy's characteristic move from quotidian detail to reflection on what lies behind that detail. The young man's youthful energy – seen in paintable face, tossing hair, "bare chest" – leads to the maxim that lover and poet, both roles for Liddy here, engage with "form adapted to the single person".

A further frame of reference lies behind the present situation: Greek experience of homosexual love between an older man and an adolescent boy. Freud's view that the Greeks loved these young boys because they possessed female characteristics and were therefore substitutes for girls[23] endorses Liddy's comparison of the young man to Marilyn Monroe and Jean Harlow.

A sublimated form of this homosexual love is described by Plato in the *Symposium* and in the *Phaedrus*, the "good read" of the poem's title. The *Phaedrus* is "Charmingly unmarginal" because its account of homosexual love functions as paradigm for modern gay men; for example, for J. A. Symonds (strongly influenced by Whitman):

> Here in the *Phaedrus* and the *Symposium* I
> discovered the true *liber amoris* [book of love] at
> last, the revelation I had been waiting for. It was just
> as though the voice of my own soul spoke to me
> through Plato, as though in some antenatal existence
> I had lived the life of a philosophical Greek lover[24]

So Liddy and partner are like the charioteer in the *Phaedrus* who represents reason and controls a horse that represents man's sensual side: "Charioteers letting go reining in". And Liddy accepts the Greek view that sexual love (*eros*) is a response to the visual, to seeing a person:

> you're in love like one
> that has caught a glint (disease)
> ... in the eye from the glinting eye

Ezra Pound held that "China is no less stimulating than Greece", and the title of Liddy's poem "You came by on bamboo stilts, playing horse .." (CP 305–06) comes from an excellent translation by Pound of a Chinese poem called "The Song of Ch'ang-kan" by the eighth century poet Li Po (called Rihaku in Japanese).[25] Pound's alternative title – "The River Merchant's Wife: A Letter" – draws attention to the fact that the line "You came by on bamboo stilts, playing horse" is used by a woman to describe how her future husband (now long away on business) first appeared before her; Liddy transfers it to a young American man.

Hence cultural renewal leads to thematic renewal. Just as Li Po appropriates earlier poets and Pound Li Po, so Liddy appropriates Pound; while Li Po deals with heterosexual love and loss, Liddy deals with homosexual love and loss ("Only in memory Pain").

What Liddy takes from Li Po is the central image of his poem, the horse (Arthur Waley's translation has no horse; Amy Lowell and Florence Ayscough weaken Liddy's title line into "riding a bamboo horse"). The horse is not that of Plato's *Phaedrus* which controls man's sensual side, but is, rather, fully involved in sexual activity; hence the image of the horse interacts with two further important images, those of kissing and of sensual water.

The horse can be a general analogue for a sexual partner, so that it symbolises the partner Liddy wishes to dominate and consume him. But mostly the horse is linked to the concept of kissing. So the kissing of men who themselves ride horses is compared to the movement of horses' hooves. Then since kissing is linked to the concept of sensual water – "I was raised on the running waters of mouths like yours" – a horse plunging into the water to bathe is assimilated to the kissing of two men. Yet a first kiss can be excessively liquid, so that a horse would not drink the water that results. Finally, a strong Greek horse from Larissa in Thessaly, source of Alexander's cavalry (the appearance of whose image on Ireland's silver half crown coin was brought about by Yeats as Chairman of the Coinage Commission)[26] is also involved in kissing:

> there mount
> the mirror for mouths

More than ordinary horses feature here: also present is the winged horse Pegasus, who created the fountain Hippocrene, sacred to the Muses, and become the symbol of artistic inspiration. Yeats had already located Pegasus in the Ireland of the revolutionary leader Pearse ("he rode our winged horse")[27] and of his own poetry ("The Fascination of What's Difficult"); he also noted that "That creature permits us to call it Pegasus, but it does not answer to that or any name".[28] Accepting this problem of nomenclature, Liddy establishes a reciprocal relationship between inspired Pegasus and inspired Ireland:

> the horse named Pegasus or whatever drank
> of real water in the ditches that sweettalked back to him

As has so often happened, Ireland and Greece are one, united here through erotic and artistic horses:

> A horse on the silver coin and now a rider.
> Grazing grass of Ireland and Greece.

The theme of China and of the Chinese poet Li Po, together with that of Yeats, recurs in three poems addressed to Liddy's long-term companion, Jim Chapson, who spent a year teaching in the province of Manchuria and whose earlier time with Liddy in New Orleans is chronicled in the poem "The Quarter" (CP 315–16). To Chapson's christian name is added the Gaelic suffix "-ín" that functions as an affectionate diminutive. The fact that these three poems are placed after two others that deal with Liddy's mother – "Epithalamion" and "Clare de Lugnasa" – stresses once more the concept that Liddy's homosexuality derives from his mother (*WT* 57–71).

The only overtly sexual poem of these three is the second – "For Jimin in Manchuria II" (CP 181–82) – whose controlling image is that of the butterfly. Often depicted on Greek sarcophagi, butterflies were the ancient symbol of the soul that changed at death from the chrysalis of the body. As Liddy stresses that a poem grows in a specific context in time, he asserts that, when Jimin flies to China, he will be with him in spirit, with prayers of the spirit ("butterfly prayers"). Conversely, the central fact back home is that, even though other sexual possibilities are available, the specific limited space of the apartment is inhabited by the absent spirit of Jimin:

> The apartment space is a butterfly
> that rustles by telling you are not
> here.

As in the poem "You came by on bamboo stilts, playing the horse ..." a frame of reference here is Yeats, section IV of whose poem "Blood and the Moon" refers to butterflies. Jimin writes poetry that provides a delicate form of prophecy like the lyrics of Yeats ("Yeats's lyric butterfly legs"); memory which is also delicate like a butterfly is the only Yeatsian mask that Liddy can manage; and Jimin is an eternally enduring soul-companion: "You are my butterfly dish, so for ever more".

Five poems given the title "Cantico" (CP 328–38) deal with Liddy's relationship with Tomás Larscheid. The short, epigrammatic lines of "Cantico per lo Túo Amore" provide Liddy's essential philosophy: what is crucial in life is bodily energy – "existing ecstasy material" – three closely-linked forms of which are sex, alcohol, and religion ("blessed by boyfriends with sex"; "(case of Blatz in the kitchen)"; "I drink out of God's wine"). For those who are not initiated, the purveyors of these forms of energy appear to be deranged:

> I am out of my mind
> the song always say to me
>
> The relatives of Jesus
> thought he was out of his mind

But Liddy, like Wilde, sees Christ as an antinomian artist who has no sympathy with dull worthies such as the Philistines, noted for mouthing the opinions of others.

From Liddy's commitment to energy stem the benedictions of "Cantico per il Tuo Amore II" and the aretalogy of "Cantico". Liddy's time with Larscheid in San Francisco, noted centre of gay love, leads him to Wordsworth's concept that:

> The thought of our past years in me doth breed
> Perpetual benediction[29]

This time is not therefore lost, but results in benedictions that are primarily directed at activities of "the uncertain body": sex, "moderate heavy drinking", "our trips to the bathroom".

The body becomes (to use a term of approval common in French critical theory) "*jouissance*", which Liddy glosses as "savor aroma cachet". But the benedictions do not ignore the anguish – real and imaginary – that is inseparable from human life: "pain and paranoia", one function of art being to chronicle these wounds: "sighing and ... singing are the same".

The final benediction is bestowed on San Francisco. Endorsed is the gay love of San Francisco, and the love of two gentlemen from Assisi,[30] the Christian charity of St. Francis and the passion of Propertius for Cynthia.

Consequently, Assisi's values are of more importance than those of the power-obsessed city of Rome, and make the love associated with St. Valentine, who is indeed buried in Rome, seem both sentimental and repressive.

What distinguishes Liddy's aretalogy in "Cantico" is that it lists *his own* virtues. Those virtues, as we might now expect, consist of participation in sex, drink, and music that recalls with relish the Sixties and Seventies. Unlike so many others, Liddy does not recant, writes no palinode; if anything, his celebration of past pleasure has become more intense.

"Cantico per Lo Tuo Amore IV" offers a further view of love: it is seen in terms of fire, its consuming force, and the ash it produces; as Yeats says:

> Have you not been paid servants in love's house
> to sweep the ashes out and keep the doors?

As we see at the end of the poem, Liddy and his lover have themselves been such lovers in the course of their various activities.

Fire can be destructive, reducing not just a Valentine card, but love itself to ashes. But fire can also be a sexual attribute of God: as Yeats's phrase "God's holy fire"[31] becomes "God's pubic fire", we draw the inference that sex is holy. It is also gay, because Yeats's martyred saints have been replaced by Cardinal Newman, noted for his "particular friendship" with the priest Ambrose St. John, whose death Newman called "the greatest affliction I have had in my life" and in whose grave he was buried.[32] Since Plutarch held that "the soul of enlightened men return to be school-masters of the living"[33] Newman is to assist Liddy in his assessment of his love, his hunger for the other.

For the contemporary homosexual poet, the theme of AIDS (Acquired Immune Deficiency Syndrome), the disease that has killed hundreds of thousands of gay men, is inescapable; Liddy's contribution is the poem "Richard Oremus" that deals with a friend who has died of AIDS (CP 321–22). The poem's title introduces a religious note, because the Latin word "Oremus" meaning "Let us pray" was used in the Tridentine Mass of the Roman Catholic Church; for example to introduce the *Pater Noster* (Our Father). This title does not say, in a conventional way, "let us pray for Richard", but addresses Richard and suggests that he and we, the readers of the poem, pray together.

Given that there are various types of Catholic, Liddy raises the ambiguous position of Christian homosexuals:

> Am I an Oscar Wilde
> W. H. Auden Catholic ...?

The answer must be "yes" because the value of each gay man's sexuality is guaranteed by the Incarnation of Christ: "Tabernaclely, these are their delectable bodies". Their sexuality is therefore not a discrete entity that can be pigeonholed and controlled by those who advocate a passive moral code, but, as Richard himself said, is a form of energy that helps produce works of art: "without sex there could be no music, no poetry". It is proper, then, that Liddy rebukes so-called Christians who regard AIDS as some kind of divine retribution by inventing his own prayer for the catalogue of those buried in the cemetery:

> Let not the
> sun do down on crowning their cruel blasphemous deaths

For as lover and artist à la Richard, his role now is to mourn.

IV

Liddy's wonderful volume *Baudelaire's Bar Flowers* (1975) validates his wish to have been Baudelaire, while engaging in a creative swerve away from the French master. As Baudelaire treats the large Romantic themes of love, death, and the transitory in *Les Fleurs du Mal* (1859), he brings to the poems an intensely urban setting and a sense of the horror of the *abyss* (*gouffre*). As a result, Valéry regards Baudelaire as highly modern:

> With Baudelaire French poetry has at last
> transcended national frontiers. It has found readers
> everywhere; it has established itself as the very
> poetry of modern times[34]

Baudelaire is also a highly sensuous poet, who presents his feelings openly; as Yeats saw, when he placed him in Phase 13 of his system, the only phase in which "can be achieved in perfection ... expression for expression's sake".[35] Hence Baudelaire regards "pleasure", which is "the torturer of souls", as a goddess to be worshipped; a goddess made very physical by Liddy as "Voluptuousness torturer of bodies" (CP 111).

Liddy's volume *Baudelaire's Bar Flowers* alters the scope, the theme, and the style of *Les Fleurs du Mal*. Liddy drastically compresses Baudelaire. The first edition of *Les Fleurs du Mal* of 1859 contained 91 poems, to which the second edition of 1861 added 35 poems, and the third edition of 1868 a further 12 poems. But Liddy's volume contains only 30 poems (together with 6 prose letters, to be taken as the equivalent of Baudelaire's prose companions to the verse poems in *Le Spleen de Paris*). Of these 30 poems, 24 relate to poems by Baudelaire, while 6 are wholly original compositions by Liddy. It is noteworthy that Liddy uses 4 of the 6 poems of Baudelaire that were condemned in 1857 as "an offence to public morality and proper habits" (this was not revoked until 1949).

The central part of Liddy's thematic swerve away from Baudelaire lies in his treatment of sexual material: while Baudelaire's concern with deviant sex relates to women such as Jeanne Duval and Marie Doubrun, Liddy substitutes a pervasive concern with gay sex (Adrienne Monnier had already identified Baudelaire's readers as *men*). Indeed Liddy's title *Baudelaire's Bar Flowers* suggests that the evil of women in Baudelaire has been replaced by the culture of gay bars, places of alcohol and of pick-ups.

Here Liddy develops the theme of isolation in Baudelaire (also admired by another homosexual, Gide), so that it refers to the sense of being different experienced by gay men, and that sense then acquires the *daemonic* force that love has in Baudelaire. As Liddy says in prose:

> The point of being homosexual ... is, I imagine, that
> you are not part of what is generally going on
>
> (BBF 39)

This difference is stressed by the fact that, after Liddy translates quite closely Baudelaire's programmatic poem "Correspondences", he immediately in his second poem – which has the same title, but relates to nothing in Baudelaire – presents gay love as different:

> this black mystery
> Of you and a few others being chosen

and involves the reader in this through the phrase "you are chosen for the works of love" (in the same way as Baudelaire's address in "Au Lecteur" to "Hypocrite lecteur – mon semblable – mon frère" – CP 104).

Drawing on Baudelaire's dictum that "Le beau est toujours bizarre", Liddy's poem ends with an image of soldiers in a bar on sexual rampage:

> The beauty demons bring does not dry up
> In fervid hearts of perverts lies The
> Church Daimonical
> The opposite of wives the murmur of evil
> The soldiers soldiers coming on.

Hence the correspondence is not between gay men and ordinary life in human symbolism (for this is several times denied); nor is the correspondence between gay men and an orthodox Church in transcendental symbolism. Rather, the transcendental correspondence is between gay men and a Church of Hell: "sex is the allegory of the pure final love that is beamed to use from infernal palaces" (BBF 12). As Sartre points out, the only sin that matters to Baudelaire is *sexual*.

Liddy's change of sexual theme is matched by a change in the register of language: sexual material left implicit in Baudelaire becomes explicit in Liddy. The most obvious example of this is the graphic use of the verb "to fuck" in its literal sexual sense (contrast the endless use of "fucking" as a meaningless, intensifying adjective in Roddy Doyle's novels). So in the poem "Les Possédés/Possessed", Baudelaire's "Je t'aime ainsi" becomes in Liddy "I fuck you like this" (BBF 29).

Liddy also modifies Baudelaire's syntax: his syntax is much closer to the non-logical syntax of Symbolist poetry than that of Baudelaire. Crucial here is Liddy's drastic reduction of punctuation, notably the omission of the commas so prevalent in Baudelaire (as in "Unsatisfied" and the first "Correspondences" – BBF 26; CP 103). The semantic significance of this non-hierarchical syntax is that it enacts in language Liddy's theme of a homosexuality that is opposed to established society.

It is clear, then, that these poems of Liddy are not translations of Baudelaire; but neither are they so loosely related to the original that they can be classified as "after Baudelaire". Rather, Liddy's poems are versions of Baudelaire that draw substantially on the content of the original, while swerving away to create something that is seriously new.

V

Most of Liddy's poems in *Baudelaire's Bar Flowers* deal with specific moments of gay or lesbian love. These poems should be viewed in the light of the poem "A Voyage to Cytherea" that presents a general view of sexual experience.

Viewed by Paglia as "one of the poems of the century",[36] "A Voyage to Cytherea" (CP 108–10) deals with the journey of the poet to the island of Cytherea off the south-east coast of Greece, which was reputed to be the birthplace of the goddess of love, Venus. In a poem of Late Romantic sado-masochism, the poet there confronts horrific sexual experience. Birds representing the malevolent violence of nature castrate a man – the poet's image – who hangs on a gibbet that symbolises the sexual guilt of Christianity (Cytherea contains no pagan priestesses for whom sex and religion are integrated):

> Fierce birds on their prey
> Were using a corpse with rage
> Each using his filthy beak
> Like a scalpel into the bloody meat
>
> Empty eyes and intestines down the thighs
> And nameless beasts
> Had castrated him and one
> Bigger than the others still clawed up.

The man's sexual fate in this "Eldorado of the fuckless" mocks the fact that in French slang "To make a voyage to Cythera" means to have sexual intercourse, endorses the view of the Spartan ephor Chilon that it would have been better if Cythera had sunk beneath the sea. But whereas Baudelaire keeps sexual experience at arm's length and ends by praying that he can avoid self-disgust, Liddy alters this ending into a prayer for sexual intimacy:

> God, make me fondle and allow fondled
> My heart and body.

A major feature of *Baudelaire's Bar Flowers* is the way Liddy adapts – in varying degree – poems of Baudelaire to homosexual themes. In some poems, the homosexual theme is briefly dealt with: in "The Death of Artists", Liddy conflates the artist with the gay man, who puts "energy into campy theses"; in "Icarus", the protagonist is contrasted with "Those who cruise the bars" (CP 107; 106).

In other poems by Liddy, the homosexual theme is more developed. So the poem "À Celle Qui Est Trop Gaie", addressed to Marie Doubrun, becomes in the end a poem about gay love. As Liddy abbreviates the original greatly, modernises the images ("highway", "car"), uses contemporary slang ("shit", "faggot"), he alters the conventional love and hate of Baudelaire into a much more radical ambivalence. Here both lovers sadistically try to poison each other, the poet seeks delight in order to overcome loathing, he wants to kill and then adore the beloved; hence Eros and Thanatos are violently yoked together. In the final strong sado-masochistic stanza, the lover with difficulty attains the body of the beloved, only to inflict great pain on an infernal person who delights in it (BBF 27):

> Soon some dangerous tropical night
> When male voluptuousness enters my thighs
> I'll slide towards you like a faggot
> Who has groped a way to Hell
> And open a gaping wound in your joyous flesh.

Another poem of Baudelaire that Liddy appropriates for homosexual love in the sonnet "The Cats" (BBF 16). Known as the poet of cats and compared by Gautier to a cat, Baudelaire sets up identifications between himself and cats, and between women and cats (in two poems called "The Cat"). Baudelaire writes that the voice of Marie Doubrun's cat – who is mysterious, seraphic, strange – "filters into my darkest thoughts", and that his eyes are directed to the cat as to a lover. Baudelaire also identifies another cat with Jeanne Duval, who possesses "a subtle air, a dangerous perfume".

Different is the poem "The Cats", made famous recently by the readings of Jacobson and Lévi-Strauss, and of Riffaterre.[37] Here the cats are seen to eliminate women and are identified with the figure of the dandy. But in Liddy's version of the poem, the cats not only eliminate women – they are "Nicer than kids in the house" – but also introduce the theme of gay men. For the cats are the friends of "special sex" and know the meaning of the term "camp": they:

> understand the beautiful camping
> Of the great sphinxes standing in the desert

Liddy has authority for linking cats to Egypt and to homosexual men. The Egyptians worshipped cats because the cat – theatrical, elegant, self-interested, cruel – "was the symbol of that fusion of the chthonian and the Apollonian which no other culture achieved",[38] and can therefore be regarded as embodying the ideal of gay love. As Wilde's aesthetic poem "The Sphinx" suggests: set in Egypt, it describes both the homosexual love of the Emperor Hadrian for the "rare young slave" Antinous and the behaviour of a "curious cat". Then the novelist E. M. Forster invokes cats to illustrate his own practice of physical homosexuality, when he writes to another homosexual novelist Forrest Reid, who refrained from physical sex: "I am for men and cats rather than boys and dogs". Finally, Liddy's fellow Irishman, the homosexual actor Micheál MacLiammóir, identified Ireland with a cat: "A feline creature, I thought, Ireland is like a cat".[39]

Four further poems of Liddy – "Possessed", "The Balcony", "Dreams of a Strange One", and "Wine of Lovers" – present us with the most overtly homosexual material in *Baudelaire's Bar Flowers*.

Liddy's version of Baudelaire's sonnet "The Possessed" (BBF 29) derives much of its force from making explicit the muted sexuality of the original and transferring it from heterosexual to homosexual love. So the male addressee is told to "take off your clothes" and "Light desire in straight country boys". So the speaker of the poem replaces the tame "Je t'aime ainsi" with the graphic "I fuck you like this". And Liddy ends his version with great homosexual power by making a Dionysiac revel out of the phrase "be what you want", and the adjectives of colour modifying night ("black") and dawn ("red"):

> Fuck when you want mad midnight or drunk dawn
> There is not a fibre in my trembling body
> Which doesn't say "Sweet Beelzebub I love you".

The universalising tendency of many of Baudelaire's poems is replaced in "The Balcony" (BBF 42) with remembrance of a specific past moment of love. Liddy's drastic compression of Baudelaire stresses the minute particulars of the occasion, which he then deromanticises by adding the consumption of alcohol and a contemporary sexual vocabulary ("titty sweet", "idolised queen"). So Liddy's final stanza changes Baudelaire's romantic kisses – infinite like those Catullus demands of Lesbia – into a modern account of gratified desire (he preserves the form of repetition that involves the device of beginning and ending a stanza with the same line):

> I know how to remember evenings fucking
> My knees trembling
> Your divine languidness
> Glistened in your soft body
> I know how to remember evenings fucking.

In "Dream of a Strange One" (CP 134), Baudelaire's peculiar man, whose exact situation is left unstated, becomes Liddy's gay man who lusts after a youth. The dream is therefore, in best Freudian fashion, made sexual, and, since the speaker abandons the gay world he has chosen, it is a dream of sexual loss. To that loss is added in the dream the further loss of death, but his death produces in Liddy a moment of sexual revelation; consequently, in Freudian terms, Eros and Thanatos are exactly joined:

> I was dead anyway. It was clear at last
> Why I had fucked so much – Is that all it
> Is.

In *Baudelaire's Bar Flowers*, the poem "Wine of Lovers" (CP 130) is distinguished by its lightness of touch, which contrasts with the more weighty tone of other poems, and by a speed produced by the very short lines. For once, love is not problematic, is indeed divine. The male lovers, newly involved and free of conventional heterosexual marriage, are so drunk on their love that they aspire to a homosexual heaven (Lesbos not being available to men). The burden of queer theory yields to simple happiness:

> Today space is terrific.
> With no wife or husband
> We'll gallop on this wine
> To a faggot heaven.
>
> Like two angel ecstatic
> With Riviera fever
> We'll reach the beach
> In the blue morning.
> On the wing of the whirlwind,

Baby,
Side by side

We'll drive up to the paradise

Of making it with someone
New.

VI

Liddy takes on board some of Baudelaire's poems about women and especially about lesbians. He notes that Baudelaire (in *The Painter of Modern Life*):

> knew that woman was more than man's mate – she is an Idol whose physical magic radiates from jewelry and make-up, dresses and under-garments
>
> (BBF 28)

But idols can be demons who deceive – as Liddy's close translation of Baudelaire's sonnet about Jeanne Duval called "Sed non satiata" suggests (BBF 26). For the Latin tag from Juvenal (6.130) refers to the sexual voracity of Messalina, wife of the Emperor Claudius, who allegedly prostituted herself all night in a brothel, but remained "unsatisfied".

Indeed the man cannot embrace or dominate this demonic being, even if he were Proserpine, Queen of Hell; for the woman's name Megaera suggests that she is both an avenging Fury and a celebrated lesbian.

Equally damning about women is Baudelaire's poem "The Poison" (CP 120), the first he wrote to Marie Doubrun. While wine and opium are agents of transformation that permit "Dark and gloomy pleasures", they cannot match the devastation wrought by Doubrun's green eyes. Transformation is now that of liquid poison that changes the male and brings him towards death: "lakes where I pervert myself".

When Liddy then becomes sexually explicit about the disastrous impact of the woman, he shows that the battle of the sexes is as much physical as it is metaphysical. The man's dreams do not "quench themselves in bitter abysses", but "crash in these bitter orgasms"; the woman's acid saliva affects not his soul, but "My morbid sex". A way out of the problem of women for the heterosexual Baudelaire is to study them as lesbians (a theme also in Balzac, Gautier, and de Latouche); indeed in the years 1845–47, Baudelaire proposed a volume of poetry with the title "les lesbiennes". Believing that it is necessary to have a heroic nature to live modernity, Baudelaire held that lesbians are heroic and so the heroines of modernity; as a result, he can identify with the lesbian Hippolyta. The significance of lesbian material for a gay man will necessarily be different: Liddy views lesbian sex as a further type of non-normal activity, practised by those who, like gay men, are not part of what is generally going on.

Three of Liddy's poems – "Condemned Women", "Lesbos", and "Delphine and Hippolyta" – deal with lesbians, the last two being among those legally condemned in 1857.

The morally impeccable title "Condemned Women" (BBF 38) is undercut by the poem's obvious enthusiasm for the lesbian loves of these female satyrs. Liddy stresses these loves by emphasising the rural pleasaunce (contrasted with the city); by omitting the comparison of the women to animals; and by introducing a spectator who does not understand what is happening.

The sexuality of these women is complex, and again calls into question the concept of compulsory heterosexuality. Their sexual feelings embrace religious fervour (pagan and Christian), sado-massochism, and a graphically described desire for physical satisfaction:

> Wearing scapulars in the dark wood
> A whip under their trailing garments
> They mix the sweat of orgasm with the tears of
>   torture.

The poem "Lesbos" (CP 121–24) chronicles the island of Lesbos in the North East Aegean that is indelibly linked with Sappho: "country of steaming slow nights" and "radiant perversions" which has "made it for fucking so much". The sexual life of Sappho resembled, mutatis mutandis, that of aristocratic men in fifth century Athens: saddled with an arranged marriage to an older man, she simultaneously engaged, as an older woman, in sexual relationships with adolescent girls. Lesbos, therefore, represents sex, where:

> kisses become whirlpools
>
> ...
>
> where slaves come on quickly
>
> ...
>
> where strange girls adoring their
> ripe bodies in front of mirrors
> caress their nudity

To the disgust of course of the puritanical Plato, who regarded sexual love (Eros) as a form of madness and deplored physical homosexuality.

In the second half of the poem, the speaker becomes Sappho herself, who, like gay men, is aware of her special nature and also of the ambivalence of bittersweet Eros:

> For Lesbos has chosen me out of everyone
> To sing the secret of these girls in flower
> I from childhood on part of the black mystery
> Unbridled laughter desperate weeping
> For Lesbos has chosen me out of everyone

No wonder, then, that Addison viewed Sappho with suspicion:

> I do not know, by the character that is given of her works, whether it is not for the benefit of mankind that they are lost. They were filled with such bewitching tenderness and rapture, that it might have been dangerous to give them a reading[40]

Liddy next exploits the late fiction that, after an unhappy affair with the man Phaon, Sappho threw herself into the sea from the promontory of Leucadia. Now Sappho herself becomes ambivalent: her drowned body is "adored" and she is "more beautiful than Venus", but she turns into male Sappho (this is originally from Horace, who regards her as competing with male poets), so that:

> Sappho who died on the day of her crime
> When insulting our rite and luxurious cult
> She gave the purple rose of sex
> To a straight guy but pride punished the impiety
> Of her who died on the day of her crime.

Nevertheless, in the final analysis, Lesbos mourns its most famous inhabitant: "From this time forward Lesbos mourns". Liddy's most powerful version of Baudelaire comes in the long poem "Delphine and Hippolyta" (CP 125–29), which relates to Balzac's novel *The Girl With Golden Eyes* and was appropriated by Verlaine in *The Girl Friend: Scenes of Sapphic Love*. Set in a dim, richly curtained room, this is a poem of lesbian love between the sexually aggressive Delphine and the young woman Hippolyta whom she seduces (the Greek names may suggest Sappho and Lesbos). Liddy captures brilliantly the luxurious post-coital setting, Delphine's self-interested advice, Hippolyta's reservations. Here is Delphine, who adopts the male role of the plough, powerful but lyrical:

> Hippolyta my sweetest love now you understand
> Do not offer the sacred holocaust
> Of your first purple roses
> To rough winds that blow them anywhere
>
> My kisses are light like the mayfly
> Hovering over great western lakes
> My kisses hollow out the grooves
> Like a tearing plough or truck.
>
> They will pass over you like the leaves
> Of a herd of cattle and horses
> Turn your azure eyes full of stars
> For one of my kisses of divine balm.

In the speech, Liddy deftly alludes to the fact that he is Irish and gay by having Delphine describe her kisses in terms of the Irish landscape:

> like the Mayfly
> Hovering over great western lakes

Just as earlier Hippolyta's lesbian love is linked to that of gay men like Bill – part image of Liddy – who reject heterosexual love and embrace art.

Hippolyta, whom Paglia identifies with Baudelaire himself,[41] feels oppressed by this new-found demonic love, but knows that Eros, the searing wind of concupiscence, will not be denied. Hippolyta puts forward her sexual program in one of the most powerful passages about sex in Irish poetry:

> I feel a gaping abyss
> Opening in my being – the abyss of my future.
>
> Nothing soothes our sexual monster
> Deep as space burning like a volcano
> Nothing cools this Fury's thirst
> Who with her torch scolds the burning wound
>
> Pull the curtains Delphine
> Let fucking bring us peace
> I wish to be destroyed in your body
> And find in your breast freshness of the grave.

As Liddy introduces the explicit words "sexual", "wound" and "fucking" into Hippolyta's address, he creates resonances with literary and psychoanalytic texts. Hippolyta's generalised fear is of the abyss she must enter, and that, of course, is quintessential Baudelaire. When she proceeds with her entry, Hippolyta's great line "let fucking bring us peace" points to what we hope to find in sex. As Mellors in Lawrence's *Lady Chatterley's Lover* finds peace: "My soul softly flaps in the little Pentecost flame with you, like the peace of fucking".[42] Equally well, such peace may not be found, because Freud points out that it may be that "something in the nature of the sexual instinct is unfavourable to the achievement of absolute gratification".[42]

Freud is again relevant to the close of Hippolyta's address: for her Eros is identical with Thanatos. The importance of that combination is stressed by the way Liddy ends his "Afterword", and so *Baudelaire's Bar Flowers*, with the theme of death by water: after voluptuous sex, "we" die in the sea. But since the sea is the symbol of matter and so of the body, it is not divorced from gay sex – as the appearance of "mermen" as opposed to "mermaids" suggests. The text tells us that we are in "Hell city"; the subtext suggests rather "a faggot heaven".

Liddy's most significant changes in "Delphine and Hippolyta" come in the last two stanzas. When Baudelaire's "The bitter sterility of your pleasure" becomes Liddy's "The white light of your demonology", the original's attack on nature has turned into praise of the sexual gods of Hell. And whereas Baudelaire orders his lesbians to flee the impossible infinite that he sees as their goal, Liddy implicitly advises gay men ("queers") to seek that infinite by fleeing the "normal". Liddy endorses gay sex, as Baudelaire could not.

For Baudelaire, women can be not only lesbians, but vampires – as in the poems "The Vampire" in "Metamorphoses of the Vampire" (BBF 40–41). Since a vampire in Baudelaire is a woman – like Jeanne Duval – who preys ruthlessly on him and since Baudelaire revels in kowtowing to her power, he exhibits a strong element of sado-masochism. This cannot apply in the same way to Liddy, who may, however, accept Baudelaire's view that woman as nature is a threatening sexual force to be bypassed by means of male homosexuality.

In the poem "Metamorphoses of a Vampire" (one of Baudelaire's favourites), the woman is a wholly destructive representative of nature, death-like, a skeleton, a virus who sucks men dry. As in the poem "The Vampire", the woman is "a carving knife", from which the poet cannot free himself.

But the apocalyptic whore of "Metamorphoses of a Vampire" exudes a most potent sexuality that Liddy's version heightens. With great eloquence this vampire corrects Dante's view that God's love keeps the heavenly bodies in place;[44] suggests that her breasts have the power to resolve opposites; and asserts that she can control disembodied angels. The concept that Eternity is in love with the productions of time never had it so good:

> Writhing like a snake on live charcoal
> Straining her breasts under her bra
> A lady gorgeous with musk she murmurs:
> "My lips are damp and I know how
> to forget respect in the depths of my bed
> I make old men giggle like children
> On my adoring breasts and for those
> Who have seen it my nude ass replaces
> The moon the sun the heavens the stars.
> Kid I am so learned in voluptuous sex
> When a man swelters in my velvet arms
> Biting my breasts that are timid dissolute
> Fragile and sturdy even the angels
> Who can't fuck would go to Hell for me".

Notes

1   Adrienne Rich, "Compulsory Heterosexuality and the Lesbian Existence", *Signs* 5, 4 (1980),

2   A. Sinfield, *Cultural Politics – Queer Reading* (London 1994), 16.

3   Allen Ginsberg, "America" in *Howl and Other Poems* (San Francisco), 34.

4   "From McDaid's to Milwaukee – Brian Arkins Interviews James Liddy", *Studies* 85(1996), 339.

5   W. B. Yeats, *Autobiographies* (London 1980), 326.

6   *The Letters of W. B. Yeats*, ed. A. Wade (London 1950), 570.

7   James Liddy, *Baudelaire's Bar Flowers* (Santa Barbara 1975), 43. Hereafter cited in the text as BBF, followed by page numbers.

8   James Liddy, *In the Slovak Bowling Alley* (Milwaukee/Dublin 1990), 24.

9   Cf. D. J. West, *Homosexuality* (Harmondsworth 1960), 140–42.

10   West (note 9), 119–20; 127–30. More recent theory discounts the impact of the mother; cf. T. Thurston, *Homosexuality and Roman Catholic Ethics* (San Francisco 1996), 105.

11   Liddy (note 4), 340.

12   James Liddy, *A White Thought in a White Shade* (Dublin 1987), 29. Hereafter cited in text as WT, followed by page numbers.

13   Catullus 61. 82–89.

14   Byron, The Bride of Abydos, Canto II, stanza 20.

15   Yeats, "Coole Park and Ballylee 1931"; Hopkins, "Epithalamion".

16   Whitman, "Starting from Paumanok".

17   Cf. R. B. Martin, *Gerard Manley Hopkins – A Very Private Life* (London 1992), 46–51.

18   *The Letters of Gerard Manley Hopkins to Robert Bridges*, ed. C. C. Abbott (1970), 155.

19   *Further Letters of Gerard Manley Hopkins*, ed C.C. Abbott (Oxford 1970), 6.

20   R. Jenkyns, *The Victorians and Ancient Greece* (Oxford 1981), 290–92.

21   *Byron's Letters and Journals*, ed. L.A. Marchant (Cambridge, Mass. 1973–77), II.6.

22   Liddy (note 4), 340.

23   Cf. Athenaeus 605 d, where the courtesan Glycera says "Boys are beautiful too, for as long a time as they look like women".

24   J. A. Symonds, quoted in L. Dowling, *Hellenism and Homosexuality in Victorian Oxford* (Ithaca/London 1996), 67.

25   Ezra Pound, quoted in P. Brooker, *A Student's Guide to the Selected Poems of Ezra Pound* (London 1979), 129; Ezra Pound, *Translations* (London 1984), 192.

26   Cf. B. Arkins, *Builders of My Soul: Greek and Roman Themes in Yeats* (Gerrards Cross/Savage 1990), 170–72.

27   Yeats, "Easter 1916"; for Yeats and Pegasus see Arkins (note 25), 87–88.

28   W.B. Yeats, *Memoirs*, ed. D. Donoghue (London 1972), 244.

29   Wordsworth, "Ode. Intimations of Immortality".

30   G. Highet, *Poets in a Landscape* (Harmondsworth 1959), 110. Yeats, *Deirdre*, regards the two men as "spiritual kinsmen".

31 Yeats, "Sailing to Byzantium".

32 Cf. I. Ker, *John Henry Newman* (Oxford 1989), Index s.v. St. John, Ambrose; Martin (note 17), 47.

33 Plutarch, *On the Daimon of Socrates* 593d–94c; W.B. Yeats, *Explorations* (London 1962), 59.

34 Valéry, quoted in M. Hamburger, *The Truth of Poetry* (Harmondworth 1972), 1.

35 W.B. Yeats, *A Vision* (London 1981), 130.

36 C. Paglia, *Sexual Personae* (London 1992), 423; pp. 421–30 deal with Baudelaire.

37 R. Jakobson and C. Lévi-Strauss in *Structuralism: A Reader*, ed. M. Lane (London 1970); M. Riffaterre in *Structuralism*, ed. J. Ehrmann (New York 197).

38 Paglia (note 35), 66; pp. 64–66 deal with cats.

39 E. M. Forster, quoted by C. Cruise in *Sex, Nation and Dissent in Irish Writing*, ed. E. Walshe (Cork 1997), 66; MacLiammóir, quoted in E. Walshe, *ibid.*, 154.

40 J. Addison, Spectator no. 223 (15 November 1711).

41 Paglia (note 35), 427.

42 D. H. Lawrence, *Lady Chatterly's Lover*, Ch. 19.

43 S. Freud, *Collected Papers* (London 1950), iv. 214.

44 Dante, *Paradiso*, Canto XXXIII.

CHAPTER FOUR

We Need Brevity:
Epigrams and Epitaphs

1

The origin of Greek epigram lies in very brief inscriptions
written on monuments that tell us whose it is, who made it,
who is buried beneath. In the Hellenistic period, epigram
became a literary genre practiced by writers like Callimachus
and Asclepiades, who dealt with erotic, literary, and
sympotic themes. These writers ensured that the hallmarks of
the genre become allusiveness, conciseness, and wit. Indeed
a central plank in Callimachus' literary programme – and one
enthusiastically embraced by Roman writers – was brevity:
"poems are sweeter for being short". Hence Horace's
assertion that "we need brevity".[1]

In Rome,[2] Ennius' epigrams grafted onto Roman forms of
expression Hellenistic features such as the elegiac couplet
metre, density of expression, the elevated status of the poet.
Catullus then uses the epigram to express an intensely
personal world, often that of love or hate. It is Martial (c. 41–
c. 104 AD)[3] who establishes the canonical model of Latin
epigram and helps to fix its subsequent form: epigram is
satirical and is part of social relationships. As Citroni says,
Martial gives epigram:

> The full dignity of an artistic instrument adapted
> to offer a realistic interpretation of the world[4]

Coleridge sums up what is involved:

> What is an epigram? A dwarfish whole
> Its body brevity, and wit its soul.

Already in Catullus, epigram may provide more than brevity and wit: it may encapsulate some matter in a very concise, concentrated way without epigrammatic wit. A mode that has been successfully exploited in recent times by Samuel Menashe.[5] Writing of Menashe, Donald Davie gets to the core of this matter:

> The poems have not been whittled down or chiselled clean of rhetoric; the rhetoric was never there[6]

II

Liddy provides us with both epigrams and concentrated poems in the volume *Art Is Not For Grown-ups* and in the chapbook *Epitaphery*. In *Art Is Not For Grown-ups* 73 out of the 91 poems (4 out of 5) have four lines or less and so exhibit the brevity of Catullus. At the same time, some of Liddy's poems – most notably the poems relating to the Corcorans – attain the concentrated non-epigrammatic style of Menashe. Liddy's three central themes in these two types of brief poems are literature, religion, and sex, with 7 out of 9 poems in *Art Is Not For Grown-ups* devoted to these themes.

Liddy's epigrams and epitaphs embrace a wide variety of moods that include introspection, celebration, and denigration. Poems of witty attack are of special interest, for it is one of Liddy's central contributions to contemporary Irish poetry to restore wit to a prominent place in it. Indeed, speaking of his recent poetry, Liddy says:

> Above all, I wished to restore humour and sarcasm to Irish poetry which was a feature of traditional Irish writing

Liddy is therefore harnessing what Witoszek and Sheeran call "the traditional of vernacular hatred", that is of lethal verbal abuse, to pour scorn on a series of Irish and American pieties. As Liddy says: "Debunking of pieties – in a sense nothing is more pious or more required of the Irish artist".[7]

The volume of Liddy's that most obviously employs wit is *Art Is Not For Grown-ups*, which is anticipated by the poem "Cracks in the Pavement" (CP 159–60). Here the target for Liddy's wit is a series of Irish pieties, which include literary pieties of various kinds. So the famous endings of Joyce's *The Dead* and of Yeats's *Cathleen Ni Houlihan* are abrasively revised in the style of the late 20th century. In the case of Joyce, we get ironic comment on Irish weather and Irish economics:

> It was wet; rain,
> not snow, was general all over Ireland
> The rain fell on the bust and the about to go bust.

In the case of Yeats, youth culture and paramilitary involvement characterise the young woman:

Peter.   Did you see an old woman going down the path?

Patrick.   I did not, but I saw a young punk rocker and she had the slouch of a bombmaker.

III

Analysis of *Art Is Not For Grown-ups* can profitably begin with the large number of epigrams about literature. To begin with, there are a number of poems about literature in general. In "Poet" (LXII) the distinguishing mark of literature, its *differentia*, is its link to sexual energy: "literature is all about kissing" and "students can still make love with poetry". Yet poetry is a verbal art: because it is circumscribed by words, what the poet celebrates is the fact of poetry being separate from the poet (unlike the organic unity of Yeats's dancer and dance).

The primal energy of literature is opposed to "puritan" theory that seeks to control how we respond to literature by abolishing choice (LXI):

> The theorist controls like
> the young bartender: he's
> a d.j. in control of the tape,
> no more jukebox, folks.

Equally well, at literary conferences that are dominated by "panels", there is much regurgitation of the banal: "Dead horses flogged" (LXXVI). And, as always, there is success and failure in writing: one man:

> won the short story competition
> in *Playboy* when he was 80
> (XXXVII);

but when the poet was looking:

> for the publisher in the pub,
> the publisher was looking for his supper
>   (II)

A large number of Liddy's epigrams deal with Irish writers, the most prominent being Samuel Beckett. Beckett appears not merely in 4 epigrams in *Art Is Not For Grown-ups*, but also in a further sequence of 12 epigrams in *She Is Far From the Land: Poems 1989–93* (CP 339–50). Specially stressed in the 4 epigrams is Beckett's well-known reticence and avoidance of publicity: "he became near-silent" (XXXII); "he hid behind the other one" (XLVIII); "he never sat for an interview" (XXXVIII). Beckett also had style: actors in his plays "wore gold paint on their bodies" (XI).

In the long sequence of epigrams about Beckett, the constant use of the Latin word *vir* in the titles has complex associations: since *vir* means "man", it suggests the notion of Beckett as Everyman; since *vir* also means "a man of courage", it suggests a very strong person (cf. Sankrit *vira* meaning "hero"). So Beckett in Paris is subject, like anyone else, to a cold and to starless cold; his Dublin Protestant world includes rats and mourning seagulls; his Socratic search for truth ends with hemlock.

But Beckett exemplifies through his avant-garde art (which suggests something Jewish in him) "heroes old age" and anticipates a new age of gold when stars may shine, an age analogous to that predicted by Anchises in Virgil, *Aeneid* 6. And reticent though he is, Beckett does take part in life through sex ("a blazing kiss"), food, and the consumption of wine that represents commitment to the present (as in Horace's *Odes)*.

All of which underlines the fundamental ambiguity of the human condition: "tree of life and gallows tree"; "let everything become mid-bay". But in this sea of matter, Beckett fully participates in nine different roles that complement each other and stress his position as Everyman.

Generous tributes are paid by Liddy to Irish writers, past and present. The enormous energy of Yeats in his work for Ireland and in recreating himself as a poet in middle age means that he "is the Hemingway of Ireland" (LVI). Austin Clarke's commitment to his poetic vocation ensured that "he put polish on being a poet for us" (LII), and the work of Padraic Colum had its special music: "the wailing of violins" (XIII). Then Kate O'Brien's dissection of middle-class life in her novels constitutes "a lilac mindfield" (XXIII), while the work of Emily Lawless at the time of the Famine "casts forth the blight" (XXI).

A further theme is the elemental in writers in Irish. The work of Máirtín Ó Direáin is like the primary element of water that Pindar calls "best" and irrigates his poetic landscape (XXXVI). Nuala Ní Dhomhnaill's use of themes such as the Earth Mother in a modern setting ensures that she "wears the diadem of the post-folkloric" (LXXIV).

Less elevated aspects of writers are also treated. Edna O'Brien is unfazed "if you were cat" (Galway slang for "terrible"). Liam O'Flaherty is distinguished because at 77 he sings in a pub:

> You'll Get Pie in the
> Sky when you die
> (LXV)

Ironic revision of Irish pieties provides the last mode of Liddy's literary poems. The Big House in general and Coole Park in particular are radically deflated: the Big House has ended up in "the Lawrence collection" and the writers in Coole must now carve their names, not on the famous tree, but "in mud" (XIV, XXVI).

Yeats, Joyce, and Heaney must also be corrected. While Yeats's injunction to "Irish poets" in "Under Ben Bulben" requires them to make use of Platonic *anamnesis* (memory) in order to write of a heroic age,[8] Liddy's injunction to those "Irish poets" is to dig deep into memory to get "to the folk poem behind" (LXVII). Joyce's famous assertion that his weapons will be "silence, exile, and cunning" is undercut by the idea that, though living in continental Europe, he remains obsessed with the Ireland he has left behind: "Hot to bogtrot" (XII). Finally, the two poems on Heaney (and "Seamus and His Kind" and "Seamus and His Kind II") are highly ambivalent: Heaney is seen to move uncertainly between nobility and bitchiness, and it is implied that his "silver spoon of the fairies" has been too easily acquired (XXV, XXX).

IV

The two other main themes in Liddy's epigrams are religion and sex. His poems about religion present a Blakean attitude that combines belief in God with scepticism about institutionalised Churches. So God is present in the central Christian drama, Mass, and in the Catholic priest who celebrates that drama (VII). So Mary, as mother of the Incarnate Word, is "beautiful" (IV). So Newman, convert to Catholicism and Cardinal, can be an exemplar (XLLIII).

In the poem "Anti-churchgoing" (LIV), Liddy attempts to get to the essence of Christ: Christ, the Anointed One, is not the accidents of life, however important they may be, but the glass that lies behind all such ephemera. Consequently, what the reverse poem "Churchgoing" (LI) privileges is Christ's paradoxical injunction to leave your family. A view that chimes with the paradoxical woman who is pro-abortion, but has a baby (LXIII).

In that family in Ireland over the centuries, you will find yoked together Christ and materialism (XLV); you will also find life attuned to the rhythms of the Church (XXXIV). A Church that must, because of the Incarnation, remain in contact with created nature and not get bogged down in "Diets and Conventions" (XX). A Church in which the theist Kerouac does not become endorsed by the State (XXXIII).

V

Liddy's epigrams about sex vary considerably in content. To begin with, there is a poem (XLVI) in which man and woman are symbolised by birds:

> A woman is a swan
> a man is a pheasant.
> The ghost of a woman is a swallow
> the ghost of a man is a curlew.

Since the origin of the pheasant by the river Phasis in Colchis suggests the voyage of Jason and the Argonauts to recover the Golden Fleece, a man becomes a heroic adventurer. Since the curlew is a long-legged wading bird (whose name suggests the French for "messenger") and since in Yeats's poem "Paudeen" the curlew's cry is divine, a man becomes a divine phallic messenger. The characteristics of a woman are very different. Since the swan is majestic, is sacred to Venus, and is the type of excellence, a woman becomes achieved in body and in character, and devoted to love. Since the swallow is a migratory bird and is the harbinger of summer, a woman becomes impossible to define exactly and a creature of passion.

Liddy can strike a note of Epicurean scorn about sexual activity (LXVI):

> What is so nice about sex
> is that it is completely meaningless

But he is also aware of the power of love's fire (1) and finds that, at boarding-school, sex is more pleasurable than singing in Church (VI):

> Kissing in the rain
> more fun than singing

Indeed Liddy requires a sexualised clergy (LIII):

> The only good Jesuit is
> one who wears a condom

A product that offers, in one word, intimations of paradise (IX): "Condom-glitter". Though not necessarily for the Irish, for whom sexual rebellion may simply result in masturbation (XXXV).

In three poems, Liddy sexualises drink, a proverb, a song. With a striking paradox (LV), he maintains that non-ecstatic, non-Bacchic involvement in sex by people who do not drink alcohol is the cause of AIDS. The Irish proverb "there is no fireside like your own fireside" becomes "there is no cock like your own cock" (L) and the song "Johnny, I hardly knew you" becomes "Johnny, I hardly blew you" (XII).

VI

The two groups of poems in *Art Is Not For Grown-ups* that have the titles "Christmas at Corcoran's" and "Mörike's 'Auf eine Christblume'" (LXX–LXXIII and LXXXIII–LXXXVI) are, in the main, concentrated, non-epigrammatic compositions. These poems are presided over by the German lyric poet Eduard Mörike (1804–1875), whose works include *Klassische Blumenlese* and whose poem "Auf eine Christblume" provides the image of the rose that dominates them. As in early Yeats, the rose is a symbol of beauty, though that beauty can be destructive. Significantly, Liddy calls Mörike "the angel of childhood" (LX) and sees in the scent of the rose "an angel hand" (LXXXV).

The two poems that best exemplify concise, non-epigrammatic composition are "Mörike's 'Auf eine Christblume'" 11(LXXXIV) and "Christmas at Corcoran's" (LXXI). Poem LXXXIV describes a unique appearance of the rose that is totally at one with the rest of nature in language that is stripped to the bare essentials (no full verb, no connectives):

> Rose not seen before
> in lovely moonlight,
> in the morning, wind-made ghost.

But in Poem LXX, the unique appearance of the rose overwhelms the rest of nature and even a human child, for its essential wildness means that:

> it
> can't live near a house
> (LXXXIII)

> Find it in a cemetary
> put it in a glass outside the window:
> like the forest lily it
> can't live near a house.

The other poems continue to see the rose as both positive and negative. Certainly, the rose can be part of pleasant music and female beauty at Christmas (LXXI, LXXIII), but the rose can also be linked to an unhappy family situation: at Christmas dinner the rose holds the tears of the poet's parents and indeed suggests the unsatisfactory love triangle recounted in Joyce's story "The Dead" (LXIX, LXXII). Finally, the rose becomes part of personal longing: when its blossoms cannot be seen, the poet goes to "search a valley for you" (LXXXVI).

VII

This chapter concludes with an analysis of what Liddy nicely calls Epitaphery. In *Art Is Not For Grown-ups*, he provides an epitaph for Kavanagh, revises that of Yeats, and writes two for himself. Then Liddy's *Epitaphery* is a chapbook containing eleven epitaphs, ten of these being for himself (one is on Kerouac).

Since Yeats believed in reincarnation, that he will come back on earth in another form after death, his epitaph revises those 18th century epitaphs that enjoin the traveller to stop and contemplate his mortality by telling the horseman to pass on regardless. In turn, Liddy revises Yeats by dwelling on the pleasure and the reality of the human cycle of life and death; this positive view results in the command to the horseman to urinate on the grave, an action which is, as Freud held, linked to sexual potency (XXIX):

> Cast a warm eye on life or death,
> horseman, piss here.

Liddy's laudatory epitaph for Kavanagh revises Yeats's version of Swift's epitaph. For what Yeats sees as Swift's Neoplatonic rest, Liddy substitutes the properly mundane and rural image of a "nest", and for Yeat's assertion of Swift:

> He
> Served human liberty

Liddy substitutes the more exacting humanism of Kavanagh's account of human poverty, of the material, sexual, and intellectual poverty chronicled in *The Great Hunger*. Here also Liddy revises himself: the fact that Kavanagh's song in the grave will include the theme of sexual deprivation requires the civilised traveller to be wary about urinating there (XXVIII):

> Patrick Kavanagh hums in his nest :
> piss here, if you dare,
> toilet-trained traveller.
> He discussed human deprivation.

Liddy has written two epitaphs for himself, the first partly undercut by its mocking title "Epitaphery", the second fully genuine. The four-line poem "Epitaphery", pays homage to those twin transformers, holy Dionysus, the god of wine, and golden Aphrodite, the goddess of love, both deities being seen as specially relevant to youth. And, while those whom the Gods love die young, Liddy is not yet prepared to die and abandon the pleasures of sex (XXVII):

> Alcohol I loved, and next to alcohol youth –
> I flirted with all, for all were worth
> my time; the pulse of hand and loins
> does not die down – and I am not ready to go.

Liddy's poem "Translate into Latin for my Epitaph" reads as follows (CP309):

> He wanted his potatoes carried through the streets
> by someone beautiful who yawned.

That the lover in question here is male is established by the fact that, while in English the phrase "someone beautiful" is gender-neutral, in Latin it must be marked as either masculine or feminine, and, in the circumstances, the choice must be masculine :

> Voluit bolbos solani suos per vias ferri
> ab aliquo pulchro qui oscitavit.

This male lover is not just physically attractive, but must possess an aristocratic nonchalance, *sprezzatura*, about his task that recalls the worlds of Alcibiades, Castiglione, Wilde. Consequently, when the theme of this beautiful lover is linked to the theme of food – both involve a kind of hunger – Liddy implies that potatoes, the staple food of the Irish poor in the 19th century and even now, can be elevated to the level of what Lévi-Strauss would call an aristocratic meal by accompanying a meat such as roast beef.[9] A beautiful male companion who participates in providing an aristocratic meal, but with nonchalance – what greater jouissance could the libidinal economy of a gay poet require?

In the chapbook *Epitaphery*, Liddy requires most of his own epitaphs to be translated into a number of different languages or dialects: dead languages such as Hebrew, Silver Latin, Old or Middle English; the Triestine dialect of Italian, the Swiss dialect of German, the Limousin dialect of French; Hiberno-English with a Dublin accent. In a deviant version of this notion one poem is to be translated into the Streets of

San Francisco. Those languages and the places associated with them often reflect the content of the epitaphs.

The first three epitaphs deal with Liddy and his mother in relation to nationalism, Catholicism, and literature. The epitaph to be translated into Old or Middle English presents the apparent paradox of two Irish nationalists like Liddy and his mother listening to the radio station of the former colonial power, England. Since Trieste inevitably suggests Joyce (who lived there from 1907 to 1915), Joyce's special brand of apostasy must lie behind the concept of Liddy and his mother being "bad" Catholics. From his mother Liddy derived his preoccupation with words: the stylistic excellence of Joyce, the incantatory rhythms of Yeats's poems, to which was added sexual liberation drawn from reading in Dublin Ginsberg's *Howl* ("I'm putting my queer shoulder to the wheel").

Appropriately, then, another member of the Beat generation, Kerouac, is granted the one epitaph not for Liddy. Here the enemy is bourgeois sentimentality which must confront the realities of sexual ambiguity, death, and bohemian living.

The most concentrated of Liddy's epitaphs, the one which encapsulates his view of youth in general, young men in particular, and America, is that to be translated into Silver Latin; a proper vehicle since the Latin of writers like Seneca is concise, dense, lapidary. Here is this epitaph and a translation by myself:

> Didn't hang out with the women except
> for an inviting faghag now and then; flew
> with youth in the Transatlantic rush/
> ruse to perpetual 22; tended to bow
> in the direction of abstention, devout
> in both misogyny and young men-worship.
>
> feminas non frequentabam praeter interdum
> blandam cinaedorum amatricem; volavi
> festinans/simulans cum iuventute trans Atlanticum
> ad XXII in perpetuum; inclinatior ad modum tenendum
> acri odio feminarum, acri cultu iuvenum.

Three other epitaphs develop the themes of the Latin one. The one untitled epitaph locates homosexual desire at the beach, where the male gaze seeks out its male object of desire; a very Greek concept, since the Greeks saw sexual desire as deriving from a visual response to physical beauty. Ironically to be translated into sober Swiss German, another epitaph deals with the famous in New York bath-houses, and a man called Nick who introduced the poet to American "epiphanies" and to "the management of desire". The epitaph to be translated into The Streets of San Francisco – a city with a large gay community – concentrates on sex (linking it to Catholicism and drink) and modifies Plato's comparison of man's sensual appetite to a winged horse by asserting that "love and sex both thoroughbreds".

In the last two epitaphs, Liddy contemplates death. That to be translated into Yola sees the poet swimming in the ocean (as his father did) and disappearing into the great primal Mother, symbol of Matter ("what's water but the generated soul?"). In the last epitaph – which is to be translated into Hebrew and suggests the insight of Old Testament prophets – Liddy on Christmas day accepts death and rebirth, in the manner of Yeats. Wishing to escape "a premonition of apocalypse" and to possess cosmic light, he prays for a return to the womb and for rebirth:

> be ready to return to my mother's womb
> for more.

We need one more epitaph before we are finished, that of the father of Latin poetry, Ennius. This epitaph offers a fitting tribute to the work of James Liddy, who, in a striking series of poems, and, in particular, in poems of wit and of sexual feeling, has now established himself as one of the most powerful and most original of contemporary Irish poets:

> nemo me lacrumis decoret neu funera fletu
> faxit. cur? Volito vivo' per ora virum.
>
> let no one honour me with tears or attend my funeral
> with weeping. Why? I fly, still living, through the mouths of
> men.

1   Callimachus, Preface to the *Aitia*; Horace, *Satires* 1.10.9.

2   For Latin epigram see M. Citroni in *Oxford Classical Dictionary*, (eds). S. Hornblower and A. Spewforth (Oxford 1996).

3   For Martial see J. P. Sullivan, *Martial: The Unexpected Classic* (Cambridge 1991).

4   Citroni (in OCD, note 2), 538.

5   For Menashe see Derek Mahon, *Journalism* (Oldcastle, County Meath 1996), 171–74. For a selection of his poems see *Penguin Modern Poets*, Vol. 7 (London 1996), 51–100.

6   Davie, quoted in Mahon (note 5), 172.

7   Liddy in *Studies* 85(1996), 337 and 340; N. Witoszek and P. Sheeran in *The Crows Behind the Plough*, ed. G. Lerreut (Amsterdam 1991), 11–27.

8   For "Under Ben Bulben" as a Platonic poem see B. Arkins, *Builders of My Soul: Greek and Roman Themes in Yeats* (Gerrards Cross 1990), 51–55.

9   For Lévi-Strauss on food see E. Leach, *Lévi-Strauss* (London 1974), 29–35.

CHAPTER FIVE

Bohemian Fiction:
Young Men Go Walking

1

Irish fiction is largely that of the outsider, the marginalised, the alienated. It is true that in the late Victorian period Irish Catholic novelists of the upper middle class (such as Rosa Mulholland) laid great stress on the virtue of their characters and their pursuit of respectable marriage.[1] It is further true that a number of later novelists such as Kate O'Brien and John Broderick depicted the daily life of the Irish bourgeoisie. And it is yet again true that a number of contemporary Irish writers such as Emma Donoghue and Katy Hayes depict the highly modernised Irish society of today.

For all that, Irish fiction has been much concerned with those who are radically opposed to the status quo. The organic society that came into existence in Ireland in the late 19th century and reached its definitive form in the first four decades of the Irish Free State was characterised by a potent cocktail of conservative politics and religion (Catholic), sexual puritanism, and a deeply authoritarian world-view.[2] Such a society had little time for the Other: dissent that came from women, the left, intellectuals, advocates of sexual freedom was suppressed. At the same time, Ireland contrived to get rid of a large number of potential dissidents by forcing them to emigrate.

In this scenario, Catholic intellectuals like George Moore and Seán O Faoláin attack various forms of bourgeois materialism and articulate a yearning for individual freedom. Moore's novel *The Lake* (1905) may serve as paradigm: the Catholic priest Oliver Gogarty, who has denounced a pregnant schoolteacher called Rose Leicester from the pulpit, comes to painfully reject his own authoritarian outlook and (after faking his suicide) leaves Ireland for a new, free life in America.

After the economic reforms of Lemass and the general liberalisation of the Western World in the 1960s, Irish society became more tolerant and outward-looking:

> Puritan Ireland's dead and gone,
> A myth of O'Connor and O Faoláin[3]

But some Irish fiction continued to represent society as authoritarian and repressed; a phenomenon dubbed by the late Augustine Martin as "inherited dissent", i.e. a mode of opposition not based on lived experience, but on uncritical acceptance of attitudes from the past.[4]

At the same time, other writers ignored public aspects of post-1960 Ireland and retreated into a private world, into an art that "located its interest in the pathology of the alienated individual".[5] Here the paradigms are Beckett, whose isolation Liddy stresses in his Vir sequence of poems (CP 339–50), and Francis Stuart, whose novel *Black List: Section H* (1971) memorably presents the isolated individual person.[6]

One mode of fiction that rejects conventional values while validating the individual outsider is the bohemian novel. The "hero" of such a novel can play fast and loose with society without finding himself in intense opposition to it; he is an outsider who has no specific blueprint for the way things should be (unlike Moore and O Faoláin), but simply wants to be able to do his own thing. As a result, the "hero" of the bohemian novel has something in common with the rogue (*picaro*) of the picaresque tradition.[7]

Examples of bohemian fiction in Ireland include Anthony Cronin's novel *The Life of Reilly*, Brendan Behan's unfinished novel *The Catacombs*, and some short stories by John Jordan (for whose own unconventional behaviour see Liddy's poem "Miles" – CP 351–52). But the most famous Irish example of the bohemian novel is J. P. Donleavy's comic masterpiece *The Ginger Man* (1955). This book relates the hilarious adventures of Sebastian Dangerfield, who is not the failed outsider of the picaresque tradition, but a disaffected middle class adventurer.[8] Rejecting the quotidian world of duty, Dangerfield operates in a parallel universe of endless gratification: much drink, much sex, no work (a scenario partly anticipated by Joyce in *Portrait* and *Ulysses*).

II

Liddy's novella *Young Men Go Walking* (1986)[9] – whose title comes from Wallace Stevens' lines:

> Young men go walking in the woods
> Hunting for the great adornment[10]

is set in Spain and in Dublin of the 1960s, which is "still a sweet Bohemian place" (YM 62). The novella explores the relationship between a homosexual teacher named Stephen Corrigan (suggestion of Stephen Dedalus) and a younger man named Vincent Cosgrave (suggestion of Joyce's Lynch, who betrayed him) and their attitudes to life and to art; these two men function as alternating narrators (in straight narrative and in letters).

The great adornment they seek has nothing to do with the newly vibrant Irish economy and everything to do with the mood of liberation that characterised the sixties. The main forms of liberation sought are drink, sex, and art, regarded as constituting life; these correspond to Liddy's "four first things" in "Kerouac's Ronsard Dance" (CP 230):

> Bacchus, Love,
> the Muses, Apollo

– the latter meaning the:

> fact of waking
> to every day.

It is largely through talk, glorious talk, that Liddy brings this bohemian life before us. Practised to perfection in the pub, talk in Ireland has a cosmic dimension: in the End was the Word. Action in comparison is of very little importance. No wonder, then, that Wilde – himself called by Yeats "the greatest talker of his time" – held of the Irish that "we are the greatest talkers since the Greeks".[11]

Bohemian life and talk needs a landscape to operate in and Kavanagh is lauded for saying "a great deal of our life has to do with inanimate nature" (YM 92). Wexford provides an example of "the heavy and sweet landscape" of Ireland:

> the county with no tales, few bogs, only pretty corners
> of rush and fern. Barley by tractor load ... Grows lush
> in summer, clumps of green greygreen and blue
> (YM 76; 86–87).

In Spain, landscape becomes an issue between Vincent and Stephen ("instinct versus artifice"). Praising unadorned nature, Vincent regards Stephen's vision of Spain and the Mediterranean as a form of tired and touristic romanticism, as a "Robert Graves subutopia". But Stephen insists on the validity of "cities, old rivers, wisdoms, culture collections", and of "the olives, the sea, the scribe in the post office". After all, "Even Shelley drank wine on the shores of the Mediterranean" (YM 111; 97–99).

So what kind of work is *Young Men Go Walking*? Liddy's classification of the novella as "a romance" that includes "A series of unusual adventures" and "a love episode" suggests a clear-cut genre (YM 76). But adventures and love in a bohemian context call to mind the picaresque as much as romance. Hence the reference to the French homosexual writer Genet who is a thief (*picaro*).[12] Hence the reference to the sexual and very carnal relationship in Donleavy's *The Ginger Man* between Sebastian Dangerfield and Miss Frost, who lets him bugger her and is therefore seen by Vincent as an analogue to be avoided (YM 68; 108).

More tellingly, the treatment of plot and of syntax expresses in formal terms the bohemian nature of *Young Men Go Walking*. This novella of less than 60 pages resolutely refuses to meet Aristotle's requirements for a plot of a beginning, middle, and end.[13] There is indeed no plot in a conventional sense; to elaborate on what was said of Beckett's *Waiting for Godot*, nothing happens more than twice.[14]

Equally well, there is little sense of an ordered society within which Liddy's characters operate. The Irish civil service, for example, appears as simply farcical (YM 86): "There's a principle behind it all somewhere but no one has found it yet". What is stressed instead is individual experience, regarded as primary. Liddy, therefore, assents to Whitman's life "One's self I sing, a simple, separate person", but rejects the line that immediately follows: "Yet utter the word democratic, the word *En-masse*".[15] Hence the hiker's interest in social progress evokes from Stephen Ovid's summing up of Orpheus' love for Eurydice, *vicit amor* (love has conquered)[16]; and the hiker's reference to agricultural work evokes from Stephen the classic bohemian response: "I never did a day's work in my life" (YM 88).

Hence Parnell is seen not in terms of politics, but in the context of the personal and sexual (YM 89).

Liddy's syntax is marked by the constant use of short staccato sentences, being couched (like the interior monologues of Leopold Bloom) in the style of the *Epistles* of the Stoic philosopher Seneca.[17] In the Late Republic at Rome, Cicero in his *Speeches* expressed a concern for public matters in elaborate periodic sentences that emphasise the connection between ideas and phrases by means of subordinate clauses and connective devices. But under the early Empire, Seneca's *Epistles* "reflect not the outside world so much as the condition and workings of his own mind",[18] and exhibit a postclassical rhetoric that makes use of short sentences; in which ideas and phrases are juxtaposed rather than connected, the sentences themselves compressed into epigram and aphorism.

Hence Liddy writes very short sentences, sometimes without a verb, sometimes without a personal pronoun. This absence of hierarchical syntax and the breaking of normal rules mirrors the way the characters break the rules of society. Indeed what absence of plot, of society, and of hierarchical syntax does is to mock the bourgeois *cosmos* and establish in its place a bohemian *chaos*.

III

In *Young Men Go Walking*, the *éminence grise* is George Moore, who chronicles modern consciousness in his fiction and in his autobiographical works, and who stresses the inner life, the soul, of the individual person; holding the view that "In Ireland men and women die without realizing any of the qualities they bring into the world" (YM 85). The importance of Moore can be grasped from the poem "George Moore and the Mermaid At the Meeting of the Waters" (WT 48–49). Intent on savouring the lush nature of Wicklow, Moore is confronted by a Mermaid who symbolises for him a future of warm Irish summers full of "steeding women". The Mermaid has the very highest regard for Moore's writing and suggests that it requires careful analysis:

> there is gold hidden under the doorstep
> of your writing.

But the Mermaid, ambiguous in shape, sees Moore as ambiguous too and as analogue for the bohemian:

> a writer of the people
> and not of the people

Moore is therefore the appropriate recipient of news of the "public disaster" the Mermaid foretells, the fact that there are no sexually available women in Ireland. So the bohemian must import them – as Francis MacNamara of the Falls Hotel in Ennistymon brought in girls from Paris (where Moore lived from 1873 to 1880), women to drink cocktails with the father-in-law of that serious drinker, Dylan Thomas.

Key concepts that emerge here are that Moore is a major writer and that he is unconventional. So Stephen is convinced that Moore will once more be highly regarded "when fashion comes round again", and notes how, though he came from a Big House, he took part in the café life of Paris with Manet and others: "Come back, George Moore's Paul Verlaine, to the café table" (YM 74; 63).

Yet Moore is not immune from criticism. Stephen feels that Moore's celebrated conversion from Catholicism to Protestantism cut him off from the mythology and mystery that is integral to the Catholic world-view, and ensured he could not be a great poet (this mystery attracted Yeats, who was a great poet). Vincent's criticism tends in the opposite direction; he feels Moore's much vaunted realism (derived in part from Zola) may not always tell it as it is: "Does he always tell what happens or who he is?" Finally, Mr. Ryan is summarily dismissive: "Young man, I know what I am talking about. Moore didn't" (YM 75).

The most sustained appearance of George Moore in the novella is when Stephen and Vincent drive from Dublin to Mayo in order to visit Moore Hall, George's ancestral house; there he frequented the stables and listened to stories instead of going to school (Moore's "stableboy childhood" – YM 78). Moore's lifelong commitment to art is assimilated to the concept of "a continuous journey" across the "impossible island" of Ireland. Indeed his passion for art and his notoriously violent temper drive Stephen to eulogy: "George Moore, you have a soul of fire" (YM 74–76). As Heraclitus says, such fire in the soul is akin to the world-fire of the Logos, from which it draws its energy and vitality.[19]

Very soon we see Moore's fiery wit in action. In a discussion of marriage, Stephen invokes Moore as an authority who spoke of "The redemption of love from the promiscuousness of marriage" (YM 77). This Blake-like dictum challenges Paul and others who regard marriage as a relief from concupiscence ("Better marry than burn"),[20] a kind of licensed fucking, and recalls Moore's attack on the Dublin marriage market in *A Drama in Muslin*. Stephen's gloss on this dictum is to assert (citing Van Gogh) that marriage stands in the way of the artist, believing that what Cyril Connolly calls "The clasping tares of domesticity" are indeed the enemy of promise.[21]

The fire in George Moore was made tragically literal when Moore Hall – "superbly Palladian in bog and mountain" – was burnt by Republic forces in February 1923, despite its owners' record as benevolent landlords. Moore's reaction was that Ireland was not a country for a gentleman, Liddy's is to declare the action unchristian: "Pagan pyre in a godless land" (YM 81; 79). Ironies about fire continue to multiply: George Moore was himself burnt, cremated, and the locals refused to row the ashes of his body across Lough Carra near Moore Hall: "Alright to burn a mansion but not the body unless it's in it" (YM 79).

But Moore had foreseen what would happen to Moore Hall in a passage (YM 81) that deeply affects both Stephen and Vincent, and that must call to mind Yeats's lines:

> Man is in love and loves what vanishes,
> What more is there to say?[22]

> Moore hall blazing amid its woods, casting a fierce light
> over the tranquil lake, lighting up the old ruins on the
> island. The lake, I said, is several hundred yards distant,
> and the water that will be pumped from it will not avail to
> quench the fire. My house will burn like a torch.
> Moreover, even if the villagers come to quench the flames,
> the Republican Army would not allow them to do so.

Everything will be lost; and I doubted not the fulfilment
of my dream; and my thoughts turning to an eighteenth-
century Dresden tea and coffee service, my heart began to
ache.

For people like Stephen and Vincent, life imitates art. The reading of Moore's prophetic passage is not merely "the communion for what is lost" in Moore Hall (YM 81), but also for what is lost in their own relationship. Stephen desires Vincent, but feels rejected by him when he engages in sexual activity with the publican's book-loving wife: "he jumped on her, me he gave the cheek, gave nothing. Cold fish, cold slug" (YM 80). As a result, the two men fight, and Stephen experiences emotional death that is assimilated to the actual death of Moore: "Moore-island dust".

One of the books owned by the publican's wife is an early edition of Joyce's *Ulysses*, whose cover is adorned with the Greek colours of blue and white. The label that Stephen produces for Joyce – "the foxiest poet of novelists" (YM 79) carries several implications. Greek colours suggest Joyce's subtle appropriation of Homer's *Odyssey*; the label implies that Joyce's etiolated poetry – acutely disparaged by Moore as "Symons"[23] – has given way to his powerful prose; and the label also points to the way that Joyce has effectively concealed the debt he owes to Moore.

For while Joyce acknowledged that the interior monologue came from Dujardin, Moore had found it there before him; and in the famous ending of "The Dead", Joyce drew heavily on Moore's story "Vain Fortune".[24] So Moore could afford to be cavalier about Joyce's masterpiece *Ulysses*: when Joyce sent him a French translation, Moore commented "It cannot be a novel, for there isn't a tree in it".[25] Hence the question in Liddy (YM 66): "Was it of the novel George Moore said it had to have a tree?" and his tentative suggestion that parodies Yeats's dictum "Irish poets, learn your trade" as "Irish novels, have you your trees?"

It is important to remember how much Moore and Yeats had in common. Both men had long careers devoted to art, heavily revised their earlier work, liked literary collaboration. Both men lived extensively in England, loved and hated Ireland, liked to visit country houses. Both men became a kind of eclectic Protestant, were keenly interested in sex, were at times very poor and very unpopular.

Nevertheless, in their respective autobiographies Moore and Yeats attacked each other vigorously.[26] Moore stresses in particular the aristocratic pretensions of the middle-class Yeats:[27]

> As soon as the applause died away, Yeats who had lately returned to us from the States with a paunch, a huge stride, and an immense fur overcoat, rose to speak. We were surprised at the change in his appearance, and could hardly believe our ears when, instead of talking to us as he used to do about the old stories come down from generation to generation he began to thunder like Ben Tillett against the middle classes, stamping his feet, working himself into a great
> temper, and all because the middle classes did not dip
> their hands into their pockets and give Lane the money he wanted for his exhibition. When he spoke the words, the middle classes, one would have thought that he was speaking against a personal foe, and we looked round asking each other with our eyes
> where on earth our Willie Yeats had picked up the strange belief that none but titled and carriage-folk could appreciate pictures. And we asked ourselves why our Willie Yeats should feel himself called upon
> to denounce his own class; millers and shipowners on
> one side, and on the other a portrait-painter of distinction ...

Hence Vincent's eulogy:

> He's unputdownable. He must have been the first to
> recognise Yeats for what he is. At that date a sign of
> genius
>> (YM 75)

IV

Stephen is a homosexual who pursues Vincent, a bisexual more interested in women. Vincent certainly has feelings for Stephen: "There's definitely a wavelength between us"; "Your love for me has become part of me". But Vincent believes that his "destiny was women" and speaks of his "permanent heterosexuality". As a result, he sees his homosexuality as "a moment's unreality" and is, for the most part, unwilling to have a physical relationship with Stephen:

> Look it, mate, I'm not your wife. I'm just a guy you
> go out drinking with.

Heterosexual sex is preferable to Greek love, to:

> a fucking Socratic dialogue in Stephen's Greek
> Temple in Grafton Street ...
>> (YM 74; 65–67; 85).

For Stephen, homosexual love is crucial, both a religion and a drug (YM 91):

> For centuries love was the dope of clerks whether
> Cathar, Renaissance, Bourbon or nineteenth-century.
> Love a secret religion.

Like Virgil (*omnia vincit amor*),[28] Stephen acknowledges the awesome power of sexual desire (YM 114): "Brains turn to sawdust in the presence of sex". But Stephen's feelings for Vincent are authentic (YM 108):

> You don't know how much – rather what ways – I
> love you. You have no idea, it's real love, not sex –
> as such.

Vincent, however, finds all this too much:

> This relationship always seems to leave you asking
> too much and me refusing
>
> (YM 97)

Nevertheless, sexual union between Stephen and Vincent takes place, its force conveyed through images that are both paradisal and Greek ("Apple. Apollo"). Vincent "tastes like an apple", the symbol of love in the Greek world, and the sun-god Apollo, the Far-Darter, is "dancing in the sky" (YM 89).

The relationship between Stephen and Vincent is inextricably linked to drink and to literature. Stephen regards drink as a religious matter – "A poet's public house is his church" (YM 63) – and attends assiduously to his religious duties. Drinking involves "the endless recycle of the pint glass" and always being about to enter a pub like Keane's "where the froth for us has already departed from a pint of Guinness and a pint of Bass" (YM 71).

For Vincent inebriation is good because it creates a more attractive way of looking at the world than the quotidian (YM 73):

> The slight drunkenness I have now from three public
> houses is the best state I can hope for because it
> distorts my vision sufficiently.

Hence Mary in McDaid's suggests that for these men the central point is to consume copious amounts of alcohol, regardless of whether it is Irish or Scotch (YM 74):

> Sean, there is a possibility at this distinguished stage
> of your career you drink too much to know the
> difference.

What brings Stephen and Vincent together is literature (YM 60):

> Chattings about writing, forms of, college love of,
> what class of imagination not possible.

Indeed Vincent is so thoroughly immersed in literature and specially in Joyce that the boundary between reality and art is blurred: an event in his own life would recall Tom Kernan's fall in Joyce's story "Grace" (YM 59). Vincent's comparison of his poems to the very weak poems of Joyce shows that even in art he tends towards the derivative and second-rate – as his brief poem "SPY WEDNESDAY" suggests (YM 59).

So it is hard to take seriously Vincent's criticism of "the standing army of Irish poets" (itself a phrase of Kavanagh's), of city poets for whom art is a substitute for sex, and of country poets who feel poetry flows "out of the mouth of a cow". Much more telling is Stephen's criticism of three other groups of poets: the formalists of Trinity College, who remain as they were at the time of Yeats's *bete noire*, Dowden; the Anglo-Irish who have tea in the Shelbourne Hotel (served as usual during the 1916 Rising);[29] and those who write in pedantic Irish – "a language that has always been retreating towards the sea" (YM 76; 70).

In the midst of all this talk of writing, Kavanagh stands out as a major contemporary figure, whose *Collected Poems* "is coming out soon" (it appeared in 1964 – YM 61). But, like other inhabitants of Bohemia, Kavanagh "lived every day without necessarily being employed or thinking of it" (YM 62). Hence his daily routine: whiskey to start the day (as an inspired poet should), a look at The Irish Times in Parson's bookshop, the pub, lunch during the holy hour (2.30–3.30), a bet on a horse (also a Dionysiac activity), the pub again.

In the end, Kavanagh was barred from the pub (the Pleiade):

> He simply told old Pleiade himself what he thought
> of him and I believe was quite expressive and
> expansive in the vulgar English and bad French (YM
> 91).

Then in November 1967 Kavanagh died. For Vincent, his loss is like that of the archetypal Dublin singer and character

Zozimus (Yeats's last gleeman): "No more Zosimus for me". But Stephen feels the loss of Kavanagh much more intensely: knowing the poet for ten years, Stephen sees him as authentic, non-academic, a drinker:

> In a city, in the one pub of a city, there was a man. Altogether different from the schoolteachers (in whose hands he will have no rest).

More: Kavanagh's apparent assertion just before he died that "I believe in God" calls to mind Kerouac's assertion that "I want God to show me his face" (YM 94–96).

Another major poet to appear in Dublin is Ezra Pound, who has close links with Irish writers: he lived with Yeats in the years 1913–16;[30] did much to ensure the publication of Joyce's work; was visited in St. Elizabeth's Hospital by Kavanagh (who calls him Longfellow's great-nephew); and Pound is linked to George Moore through the image of fire: "The masculine fire of the *Cantos*" (YM 84). Finally, Stephen parodies Pound's line "What thou lovest well shall not be reft from thee" in the context of a gay bar: "What thou lovest well stays on the jukebox" (YM 116).[31]

Pound attended the funeral in Westminster Abbey in 1965 of T. S. Eliot, whom he called "the true Dantescan voice" and whom Vincent labels "Uno anglo-Catolico" (YM 102). Pound then went on to Dublin to visit Yeats's widow George; it seems he also wished to see Kavanagh (and Austin Clarke).[32] The reaction of the Dublin literati to Pound's unexpected presence is to send a vigorous telegram (YM 84): "Irish writers say with pride a welcome to Yeats's and Joyce's city and ours". They also praise Pound. Vincent calls him "a greater stud than any languishing stud on this here stud farm". Garland's assertion that "he has the taste of Italy and the whole of antiquity in his mouth" calls to mind Pound's *Homage to Sextus Propertius,*[33] his translation of Sophocles' *The Women of Trachis*, his use of Dionysus in the *Cantos*, his commitment to Italy (however misplaced).

But there is a considerable gulf between Pound and Mrs. Yeats and these writers. Pound, unlike them, does not believe that "the imagination was helped by alcohol". George Yeats is said to despise the Yeats Summer School in Sligo and to have closed down the Cuala Press "because there was nothing worth publishing". So it is no surprise that the telegram "will not be remembered" (YM 83–84).

Literature is also a topic when Stephen goes to Spain – "they love poetry here too" (YM 102) – the two key figures being Machado and Lorca. Stephen carries the Penguin Lorca around with him, notes of Valladolid that "Garcia Lorca walked through it in the twenties", and even sees in a dream the poet's "lost *Sonetas del amor oscuro*" (YM 110; 101; 94). Stephen also sees Lorca (murdered by Fascist forces) as equating language and woman in a way Franco could not:

> At Hendaye he heard Spanish being spoken, like
> the voice of woman he loves. Franco never wrote
> like that, Lorca did
> (YM 93)

But in Spain Machado is specially prized: "All learn the greatness of the same poet and believe it. Lorca second-class". So Manolo "knows Machado is the one" and Stephen finds Machado's Spain in Zamora: "very quiet old cafés, shoeshiners, papers" (YM 102, 97). But when Stephen recites Lorca's "Ode to the Blassed Sacrament of the Altar" to a group of poets, the conventional estimate has to be revised:

> None of them can say for that moment that
> Machado was greater than Lorca. I have silenced
> Spain on its own ground
> (YM 104).

At the end of *Young Men Go Walking* (116–17), Stephen reaffirms his commitment to the bohemian life: a life of drink, sex, idleness in a romantic landscape with great talk. So Stephen sees the real landscape of Spain as "Peaches, oranges, roads, sweeping bends, sudden olive orchards" and a "fisherman's bar at the harbour". So Stephen, after ribald talk, has sex with a man who has been rejected by women and, as usual, sees this in terms of apples (YM 116–17).

Experiences Stephen can enjoy because his victory in the form of a day of idleness replaces Julius Caesar's military victory at the battle of Zela in 47 B.C. (*vici*): "Another day idled. I have conquered". As earlier in Cordoba in the Calle de Munda, named after another victory of Caesar there in 45 B.C., Vincent and Stephen found "the most perfect bar in the world" (YM 117; 110).

For Stephen, there is one story and one story only (likely to appeal to the absent Vincent). As Stephen employs functional conversion[34] by making the Gaelic noun "shebeen" into a verb, he posits an idyllic scenario of drink in a small pub, of art that does not die, of fairies that may be supernatural or human male: "shebeening to the immortal music of the shee". As with the Spanish picaresque novel, this is a world of *burlas y veras*, of jests and truths.[35]

Notes

1   J. W. Murphy, *Catholic Fiction and Social Reality in Ireland 1873–1922* (Westport, Conn./London 1997), 25–37.

2   B. Arkins, "The Closing of the Irish Mind – Ireland Since 1922", *Planet* 103(Feb/Mar 1994), 48–61.

3   John Montague, "The Siege of Mullingar, 1963".

4   A. Martin, "Inherited Dissent: The Dilemma of the Irish Writer" in his *Bearing Witness – Essays on Anglo-Irish Literature* ed. A. Roche (Dublin 1996), 81–99; review by B. Arkins, *Studies* 86(1997), 87–89.

5   D. Kiberd, *Inventing Ireland* (London 1995), 584.

6   Stuart is close to the sort of mentality described by C. Wilson, *The Outsider* (London 1963).

7   For the picaresque novel see H. Sieber, *The Picaresque* (London 1977).

8   Sieber (note 7), 70–72.

9   James Liddy, *Young Men Go Walking* in *Triad – Modern Irish Fiction* (Dublin 1986), 57–117. Hereafter cited in the text as YM with page numbers.

10 Wallace Stevens, "The Pediment of Appearance".

11 W. B. Yeats, *Autobiographies* (London 1980), 139; 135.

12 For Genet's relation to the picaresque see Sieber (note 7), 67.

13 Aristotle, *Poetics* 7.

14 V. Mercier, described *Waiting for Godot* as a work in which "nothing happens, twice" [quoted in P. Murray, *The Tragic Comedian* (Cork 1970), 85].

15 Walt Whitman.

16 Ovid, *Metamorphoses* 10.26.

17 H. Kenner, *Dublin's Joyce* (New York 1987), 214–24.

18 M. Wilson, *Ramus* 16(1987), 103.

19 Heraclitus, frs. 36; 118.

20 Paul, 1 *Corinthians* 7:9.

21   C. Connolly, *Enemies of Promise* (Harmondsworth 1961), 125; he deals with marriage at pp. 125–28.

22   George Moore, *Conversations in Ebury Street*, Chapter XX; Yeats, "Nineteen Hundred and Nineteen".

23   R. Ellmann, *James Joyce* (Oxford 1983), 135.

24   W. F. Blissett, "George Moore and Literary Wagnerism" in *George Moore's Mind and Art*, (ed.) G. Owens (Edinburgh 1968) 73; Ellmann (note 22) 358; 250.

25   Ellmann (note 22), 618.

26   B. Arkins, "Writing the Hostile Self: Autobiography in Moore and Yeats", *Ropes* 5 (1997), 46–48.

27   George Moore, *Hail and Farewell*, ed. R.A. Love (Gerrards Cross 1985), 540.

28   Virgil, *Eclogues* 10.69.

29   Elizabeth Bowen, *The Shelbourne* (London 1951), 128.

30   A. W. Litz, "Pound and Yeats – The Road to Stone Cottage" in *Ezra Pound Among the Poets*, ed. G. Bornstein (Chicago/London 1985), 128–48; J. B. Longenbach, *Stone Cottage: Pound, Yeats, and Modernism* (New York 1988).

31   Ezra Pound, *Canto* LXXXI.

32   H. Carpenter, *A Serious Character – Life of Ezra Pound* (London 1988), 887–88.

33   B. Arkins, "Pound's Propertius: What Kind of Homage?" *Paideuma* 17(1988), 29–44.

34   For this device in Hopkins see B. Arkins, *Studies* 86 (1997), 141–42.

35   A 17th century critic of a Spanish picaresque novel, quoted by Sieber (note 7), 3–4.

EPILOGUE

I

Liddy's volume *Gold Set Dancing*,[1] published in July 2000, is, for the most part, concerned with topics that have been addressed previously in this book, and could indeed be regarded as his *summa*. What Liddy presents us with (in settings that are nearly always in Ireland or in America) is that mixture of the special and the quotidian that he has made uniquely his.

Hence there are poems that deal with writers who are both Irish and American, and poems that tell about ordinary people in Ireland and in America. Irish writers who pervade the volume include some writing in English like Yeats, Kavanagh, and Friel, and others writing in Irish like Raftery, MacLiammóir, and O Riordáin; the sprinkling of American writers includes Fitzgerald, Stevens, and Kerouac. There are poems about people Liddy knows in Ireland, including his grandparents, the publican Vince O'Rafferty, and his friends Tom and Nora; other poems deal with gay lovers in America. Lastly, there are poems that relate to the rural landscape in Ireland (notably Clare) and to the urban landscape in America (notably Milwaukee), while satire is represented by the poem "A Keening".

II

Analysis of the poems in *Gold Set Dancing* may begin with those that deal with Irish and American writers.

Because Liddy's own voice is so distinctive, he can come to terms with Yeats and avoid the anxiety of influence (as experienced by Clarke and others); sure of Yeats's greatness, but not in awe of it, Liddy can afford sardonic irreverence:

> At 60 you join the yacht club
> and go sailing to Byzantium
>
> (*GSD* 21)

Similarly, the poem "The Apparitions" (*GSD*) turns the death-like apparitions of Yeats's poem of the same title into a bevy of Irish poets at Thoor Ballylee, who tend towards the Yeatsian hieratic and who are ironically equated with the executed leaders of the Easter Rising in a further Yeats poem "Sixteen Dead Men": "Sixteen poets (sixteen dead men?)".[2]

Liddy's mentor Kavanagh appears, when his lines about fulfilling water –

> a barge comes bringing from Athy
> And other far-flung towns mythologies[3]

– are referred to in a dream about Jack Yeats at a nursing home on the canal, and adapted to involve Yeats in a potentially fruitful relationship with the archetypal queen Cleopatra that symbolises the mythic nature of the painter's Irish landscapes (*GSD* 26).

In commenting on Brian Friel's play *Wonderful Tennessee* (1993),[4] Liddy notes that the *dramatis personae* are "middle-aged failures on stage". But in keeping with the links to Greek and Christian religion enjoyed by the play's mysterious island, Liddy also espouses the idea (beloved of A.E.) that divine forces are returning to Ireland; and he wonders whether the character Frank who arranges stones on the pier at the end of the play may be "in the image of Christ" (*GSD* 19).

Two writers in Irish who feature in *Gold Set Dancing* have roots in the West of Ireland, Raftery and Padraig O Conaire. Knowledge of Raftery's poems is seen to have a physical impact upon the earth (*GSD* 8):

Thanks to him and his fiddle
the children preserve the landscape
by instilling some of his lines

There is praise too for Padraig O Conaire, whose statue is in Eyre Square in Galway and who wrote a book called *M'Asal Beag Dubh* (My Little Black Donkey):

The donkey taught
O Conaire how to partake
so that he could turn poetry into prose
(*GSD* 17)

Liddy identifies with the great actor and author Micheál MacLiammóir, who was:

tempermental, brilliant, exceptionally intelligent and intuitive, socially adroit, histrionic, multilingual and multi-gifted, with a genuine visual flair.[5]

Liddy asserts that MacLiammóir, who is conceived of as a possible "lark", was born neither in London (the reality) nor in Cork (the fiction), but "on that patch of earth named to poetry". Living in Galway in the 1920s and author of a play called *by Moonlight*, MacLiammóir was keen on pretty boys:

Moonlight marches on the Salmon Weir
boys, MacLiammóir's vision (1938)
(GSD 17–18)

Liddy's poem for Sean O Riordáin pays the Gaelic writer a striking tribute precisely because he combines and equates three of his own central preoccupations, drink, sex, and poetry. Since these are forms of energy, O Riordáin is regarded as exuding energy (*GSD* 13).

Coming to American writers, we find Liddy referring to Wallace Stevens in order to distance himself from the chronicler of supreme fictions and to suggest that his own brief account of landscape may have an acid flavour (*GSD* 7):

Wallace Stevens en poeme
on the High Cliffs of Moher, note:
my postcard will be different, maybe sour.

The Beat generation also continues to feature in Liddy's work. Since Kerouac functions (as often) as an exemplar of leisure (*otium*) and of belief in a benevolent God, he is quoted by Liddy, who is teaching *Dharma Bums*:

> Why don't you just relax
> and enjoy God?

Kerouac further exemplifies the energy of travel and of partying, so that he goes down the "road of endless pirouetting", and so that he "could have danced all night (*GSD* 64–64). But Kerouac, like so many, becomes fodder for academic discourse as:

> waiters and waitresses
> who go to college
> write papers on food references in Dharma Bums

Finally, Kerouac was prefigured in spectacular fashion by the Jazz Age of Scott Fitzgerald, who was "the lead singer of the band" (*GSD* 66).

III

People and places in Ireland are important in *Gold Set Dancing*. The very first poem of the volume links Liddy's mother Clare to his long-term partner Jim Chapson in a significant way because the scenario in which Jim photographs Clare's dolls suggests "some new haven" (*GSD* 3).

Liddy presents an elaborate treatment of his grandparents on both sides in section II of *Gold Set Dancing* (35–48) that consists of three prose poems and one in verse. The prose poems are written in a taut style that often omits verbs and so stresses objects (nouns), with the result that Liddy (like Joyce) lists things as though he (or Aristotle) had just enmattered their essence; at the same time, more magical worlds exist simultaneously with the quotidian, demonstrating Liddy's pervasive intermingling of the ordinary and the extraordinary. So the Ireland of his grandparents experiences desperate poverty –

> by the side of the house hundreds of people,
> unwashed unshaven in near-rags or poor clothes,
> walking up with a sour look or a drunk look on
> their faces

– but also artistic endeavour:

> Mammy says that's Lord and Lady Longford,
> who have a theatre on tour
> (*GSD* 45–46)

So the elaborate account of his mother's grandparents asserts that:

> The driveway is a slope, almost a little hill, it pours
> out onto the road on which transit cattle, horses,
> sheep; and bicycles unwashed, unwashable

but also refers to the vital Biddy Early, who "can give people anything" (GSD 38).

Without any of the anxieties that attend MacNeice's poem "Prayer Before Birth",[6] Liddy in the poem "Mass of Christmas Eve" (*GSD* 47–48) writes of his own origins in the marriage of his parents on Christmas Eve, 1931. Central to the poem is the figure of Christ, whose birthday follows the next day, and who is viewed as "a complex unity". Just as Christ is the Alpha and the Omega, the beginning and the end, so his parents' marriage represents for Liddy "a river that begins on Christmas Day", while this potential human being "sings a song with an end". Christ must be offered what Liddy calls "Prayeroics" (a calque on words like "heroics"), because of his real presence in the Mass that inspires wonder turning into a kind of dream (*Songe*), but one which provides the energy to launch human endeavour. At the same time, Christ is all that is human – "whatever drifts out there on the sea" – and this humanity reminds us of the inevitable fact of death: "A skull hovers over water which is a new day".

Liddy's two elegies for the public Vince O'Rafferty (*GSD* 27–33) concentrate more on the man's life and achievements than on loss, stressing the three aspects of drink, music, and Classical learning. Inevitably, an elegy for a publican involves praise of drink, of "whiskey fire in the night"; as Liddy writes of another man:

> he didn't so much
> like his whiskey as he couldn't be kept from it
> (*GSD* 23)

But the chief topics of "Elegy for a Publican" are praise of Vince's playing of the accordion and his rootedness in Greek and Latin culture. Vince plays numerous songs such as *The West's Awake*, *On Raglan Road*, and *The Croppy Boys*, so that:

> He is playing accordion in bar closing time
> which goes on forever in a village

Vince's use of "classical lines and tags" is seen as part of immemorial Irish tradition:

> the product of a thousand hedge schools
> and seminarian centuries

The result is that he himself becomes "Bacchus in the lounge", while Liddy can use the famous closing line of Catullus' elegy for his dead brother to write of this classically-minded musician:

> Ave atque Vale,
> poeta milesque (of the squeeze box)

The landscape of the West of Ireland, of Clare and Galway appears in the poems "West Clare" and "Tribal City" (*GSD* 6; 16–17). Summer in Kilkee sees the poet seeking after the "mortal bodies" of "young/Armada sailors", so that he becomes "a queen of the golden west", and so that West Clare is seen to mirror Provence's stress on love.

Galway's designation as "the city of the tribes" gives Liddy the title for his poem "Tribal City". Like much in Liddy, this poem stresses the centrality of the human body –

"All flesh should sob with our flesh" – while adverting to Galway's recent renaissance:

> I stroll of course in old sunshine
> while watching a new hive ... the Celtic veldt
> stretches out

But Galway has always accommodated those from elsewhere, so that the tribes include not just "the Lynchs of Barna House" and the MacDonagh's ("the best fish and chips"), but also Padraic O Conaire from Connemara and Micheál MacLiammóir from London.

IV

The themes of gay love and of satire also appear *in Gold Set Dancing* (the latter just briefly).

To understand gay love, it is necessary to understand men, and Liddy gives us the key in the poem "What I Believe About Men" (*GSD* 69). The one requirement for a man (which Catholicism must take on board) is to "do everything for the sake of what it is". The setting for men like this who indulge in gay love is, inevitably, America, so that in San Francisco Liddy experiences "mouths, limbs, kiss-talking" (*GSD* 52).

What dominates the short poem about a boy called "Casey's Light" (*GSD* 72) is the Indo-European word "light" that occurs 6 times in 25 lines. The opening lines suggest that Casey's Light has links to the divine, so that its intensity makes "you feel surpassed". So the first words of the poem "Light made" suggest the concept "And God said, Let there be light, and there was light" (Genesis 1:3), while the statement "light is a star attraction" suggests the further concept that Christ is "a light that shines in the dark" (John 1:5). Furthermore, when light is viewed as a thirst for life – as in buying a car or a farm – it recalls the equation in Classical Greek of light (*phos*) and life.

This sort of light has other properties. It is not self-centred ("doesn't masturbate"); although voracious, it is good for "tender hearts"; and, for all its divinity, it is also (like Christ) fully human, "trash that stays trash", and provides material for poets. Finally, this sort of light reverses the way we look at the world: instead of there being:

> something rotten in the state of Denmark
>
> …
>
> light marches in
> and through Denmark

The poem "The Street is Great" (*GSD* 71) firmly locates the complex interconnections between two male lovers in an urban setting. The way the two men connect is so intense that it defies the rules of logic:

> I address a letter to you as I drive
> you give me a call as I am driven

Such love is, of necessity, antinomian: "Love is an orphan driving an unlicensed car". And that car is the key to living in the city:

> Love drives
> in a Saab with an open roof
> on hot summer days in the city

Gay love can be complicated when Liddy finds that "(I'm in love with a man who's just married)", and quotes Catullus' epithalamion for his friend Manlius (61) to assert that the bridegroom is "no less beautiful" than the bride. But Liddy shows great generosity of spirit about the married couple: he unites for them epithalamia in which Nora is "synonymous with apotheosis", and in which the Roman marriage god Hymenaeus (again out of Catullus 61) is "come to marry them" (*GSD* 53–56). Furthermore, Liddy writes for the couple a lyrical hymn to Venice, seat of love in all its multifarious guises (*GSD* 57). Liddy has therefore earned this sentiment about women:

> Time to clip the ears off the donkey of misogymy
> and send him to a ruined church-island off the coast
>
> (*GSD* 70)

If the poem about Venice is a hymn of praise, then "A Keening" (*GSD* 11–12) is a series 39 of curses that are in each case introduced by the word "may", which expresses a wish and is followed by the infinitive. Involved here is the steady stripping away of all the various props upon which human beings depend, family, nature, religion, politics, art. As the last two curses summarise:

> May the Real Presence give you presence
> May Faith produce Fate

V

This brief analysis of *Gold Set Dancing* may fittingly conclude by invoking Nietzsche's categories of the Dionysius and the Apollonian. When Liddy refers to "my disease brilliant attacks of exaggeration" (*GSD* 51), it is clearly Dionysus who presides; as Liddy says elsewhere, "boldness is all",[7] and it is clearly necessary if poetry (and life) are not to succumb to the endlessly banal. But this Dionysiac tendency is balanced by an Apollonian concern with ordinary existence:

> The silver and gold of my own mind,
> and the half-bliss of ordinary life
>
> (*GSD* 15)

This nexus of attitudes can be transposed into religious terms other than Greek. Liddy is a theist, and, as with Hopkins, his poems about the material world celebrate God: "Laudamus Te" (*GSD* 7). Indeed Liddy notes that created matter like the Byzantine gold admired by Yeats (another confirmed theist):

> is from the cup where
> Christ's blood flowed
>
> (GSD 21)

But Liddy also accepts the radical implications of the Incarnation: "And the Logos became flesh and pitched his tent among us" (John 1:14). Hence God is seen as endorsing drink and sex:

> Our party art on earth
> hallowed be thy glasses
>
> …
>
> Eros fires the mind
> even more powerfully
>
> (*GSD* 25; 58)

Finally, Liddy's glorious oxymoron "the immortal shite of the heart" (*GSD* 61) sums up much in his work. Here both language and theme involve *jouissance*. Linguistic pleasure comes from the way in which the juxtaposition of the Latin-based adjective "immortal" and the Anglo-Saxon noun "shite" is mediated by the Indo-European root of the noun "heart". Thematic pleasure comes from the way in which despised excrement is derived not from the anus, but the heart, and from the way in which, far from being just waste, it overcomes death. In the end, both Hopkins and Liddy remain conscious of human weakness and human glory, but there is a difference of emphasis. Hopkins stresses the pathetic nature of man – "This Jack, joke, poor potsherd, patch, matchwood" – before acknowledging that he is "immortal diamond". Liddy does not linger on that pathetic aspect of man, but renders it "immortal" straightaway. Which gives us a poetry of such radical Incarnationalism that it can appeal, in equal measure, to theist and atheist alike. Te, Jacobe, laudamus.

Notes

1. James Liddy, *Gold Set Dancing* (Cliffs of Moher 2000). Herafter cited in the text as GSD, followed by page number.

2. *W. B. Yeats: The Poems*, ed. R. Finneran (Dublin 1984), 193–94; 344.

3. Patrick Kavanagh, *Collected Poems* (London 1972), 150.

4. Brian Friel, *Wonderful Tennessee* (Oldcastle 1996).

5. B. Fallon, *An Age of Innocence: Irish Culture 1930–1960* (Dublin 1998), 142.

6. *The Collected Poems of Louis MacNeice*, ed. E.R. Dodds (London 1979), 193–94.

7. "From McDaid's to Milwaukee: Brian Arkins Interviews James Liddy", *Studies* 85 (1996), 340.

Select Bibliography

WORKS BY JAMES LIDDY

In a Blue Smoke (Dublin 1964)

Blue Mountain (Dublin 1968)

Baudelaire's Bar Flowers (Santa Barbara 1975)

Corca Bascainn (Dublin 1979)

At the Grave of Father Sweetman (Dublin 1984)

You Can't Jog for Jesus: Jack Kerouac as a Religious Writer (Milwaukee 1985)

Young Men Go Walking in *Triad: Modern Irish Fiction* (Dublin 1986)

A White Thought in a White Shade (Dublin 1987)

In the Slovak Bowling Alley (Dublin 1990)

Art Is Not for Grown Ups (Milwaukee/Dublin 1990)

Trees Warmer Than Green (Laois 1991)

Collected Poems (Omaha 1994)

'Patrick Kavanagh and the Beat Generation' in *Patrick Kavanagh*, (eds). K. R. Collins, J. Liddy, E. Wall (Omaha 1995), 30—36.

Epitaphery (San Francisco 1997)

Poets in a Frieze and a Valentine (New York 1999)

Gold Set Dancing (Cliffs of Moher 2000)

WORKS ABOUT JAMES LIDDY

Arkins, B., Introduction to James Liddy, *Collected Poems* (Omaha 1994), 1—17.

— 'From McDaid's to Milwaukee — Brian Arkins Interviews James Liddy', *Studies* 85 (1996), 334—40.

— 'From McDaid's to Milwaukee: The Poetry of James Liddy', *Etudes Irlandaises,* 23 (1988), 67—90.

Egan, Desmond, Review of James Liddy *A White Thought in a White Shade,* Studies 77 (1988), 107.

Skinner, K., 'James Liddy's Blues: The Early Poetry', New Series: *Departures* 1 (1996), 52—60.

Stanley, G., 'Beyond the Sublime: Reading James Liddy', *Irish University Review* 28 (1998), 92—109.

Tobin, D., *North Dakota Quarterly* (Spring 1999), 116—24.

OTHER WORKS CITED

Altman, D., *The Homosexualisation of America and the Americanisation of Homosexuality* (Boston 1982)

Arkins, B., 'Pound's Propertius: What Kind of Homage?' *Paideuma* 17 (1988), 29—44.

— 'Thucydides and Lough Owel: Interview with Desmond Egan', *Etudes Irlandaises* 14, 2 (1989)

— *Builders of My Soul: Greek and Roman Themes in Yeats* (Gerrards Cross 1990)

— *Desmond Egan — A Critical Study* (Little Rock 1992)

— 'The Closing of the Irish Mind: Ireland Since 1922', *Planet* 103 (Feb—Mar 1994), 48—61.

— 'Great Hunger, Some Room: Kavanagh and Irish Society' in *Patrick Kavanagh,* (eds). K. R. Collins, J. Liddy, E. Wall (Omaha 1995), 3—18.

— Review of A. Martin, *Bearing Witness: Essays on Anglo-Irish Literature,* ed. A. Roche (Dublin 1996), *Studies* 86 (1997), 87—89.

— 'Writing the Hostile Self: Autobiography in Moore and Yeats', *Ropes* 5 (1997), 46—48.

Blissett, W. E., 'George Moore and Literary Wagnarism' *in George Moore's Mind and Art,* (ed.) G. Owens (Edinburgh 1968), 53—76.

Bloom, H., *Yeats* (Oxford 1970)

— *The Anxiety of Influence* (Oxford 1975)

Borges, J. L., *Labyrinths* (New York 1964)

Bowen, E., *The Shelbourne* (London 1951)

Brooker, P., *A Student's Guide to the Selected Poems of Ezra Pound* (London 1979)

Byron, Lord, *Letters and Journals,* (ed.) L.A. Marchat (Cambridge, Mass. 1973–77)

Carpenter, H., *A Serious Character — Life of Ezra Pound* (London 1988)

Commager, S., *The Odes of Horace* (New Haven 1962)

Connolly, C., *Enemies of Promise* (Harmondsworth 1961)

Cronin, A., *Dead as Doornails* (Dublin 1980)

Dowling, L., *Hellenism and Homosexuality in Victorian Oxford* (Ithaca/London 1996)

Ehrmann, J. (ed.), *Structuralism* (New York 1970)

Ellmann, R., *James Joyce* (Oxford 1982)

— *Ulysses on the Liffey* (London 1984)

Foster, R., *Modern Ireland 1600–1972* (London 1989)

Freud, S., *Collected Papers* (London 1950)

Ginsberg, Allen, *Howl and Other Poems* (San Francisco)

Hamburger, M., *The Truth of Poetry* (Harmondsworth 1972)

Higlet, G., *Poets in a Landscape* (Harmondsworth 1959)

The Letters of Gerard Manley Hopkins to Robert Bridges, (ed.) C. C. Abbott (1970)

Further Letters of Gerard Manley Hopkins, (ed.) C.C. Abbott (Oxford 1970)

Hornblower, S. & Spewforth, P., *Oxford Classical Dictionary* (Oxford 1996)

Jenkyns, R., *The Victorians and Ancient Greece* (Oxfoard 1981)

Kavanagh, Patrick, *Collected Prose* (London 1967)

Kenner, H., *Dublin's Joyce* (New York 1987)

Ker, I., *John Henry Newman* (Oxford 1989)

Kiberd, D., *Inventing Ireland* (London 1995)

Lane, M. (ed.), *Structuralism: A Reader* (London 1970)

Lawrence, D. H., *Lady Chatterley's Lover* (London 1932)

Leach, E., *Levi-Strauss* (London 1974)

Lerreut, G. (ed.), *The Crows Behind the Plough* (Amsterdam 1991)

Litz, P., 'Pound and Yeats: The Road to Stone *Cottage' In Ezra Pound Among the Poets,* ed. G. Bornstein (Chicago/London 1985), 128—48.

Longenbach, J. B., Stone Cottage: Pound, Yeats, and Modernism (New York 1988)

MacNeice, L., *Modern Poetry* (London 1933)

Mahon, Derek, *Journalism* (Oldcastle 1996)

Martin, A., *Bearing Witness: Essays on Anglo-Irish Literature,* ed. A. Roche (Dublin 1996)

Martin, R. B., *Gerard Manley Hopkins: A Very Private Life* (London 1992)

Menashe, Samuel in *Penguin Modern Poets,* Vol. 7 (London 1996), 51—100.

Meyers, J., *Homosexuality and Literature 1890—1930* (London 1987)

Moore, George, *Hail and Farewell,* (ed.) R. A. Cove (Gerrards Cross 1985)

Murphy, J. W., *Catholic Fiction and Social Reality in Ireland 1873—1922* (Westport, Conn./London 1997)

Murray, P., *The Tragic Comedian* (Cork 1970)

Nicosia, G., *Memory Babe* (Berkeley 1994)

Paglia, C., *Sexual Personae* (London 1992)

Pound, Ezra, *Translations* (London 1984)

Rich, P., 'Compulsory Heterosexuality and the Lesbian Existence', *Signs* 5, 4 (1980)

Sheeran, P., 'Genius Fabulae: The Irish Sense of Place', *Irish University Review* 18 (1988), 191—206.

Sieber, W., *The Picaresque* (London 1977)

Sinfield, A., *Cultural Politics — Queer Reading* (London 1994)

Sullivan, A., *Virtually Normal* (New York 1995)

Sullivan, J. P., *Martial — The Unexpected Classic* (Cambridge 1991)

Thurston, T., *Homosexuality and Roman Catholic Ethics* (San Francisco 1996)

Walshe, E. (ed.), *Sex, Nationality and Dissent in Irish Writing* (Cork 1997)

West, R. J., *Homosexuality* (Harmondsworth 1960)

Wilson, C., *The Outsider* (London 1963)

Wilson, M., 'Seneca's Epistles to Lucilius: A Revaluation', *Ramus* 16 (1987), 102—21.

Yeats, W. B., *Autobiographies* (London 1980)

— *Essays and Introductions* (London 1961)

— *Explorations* (London 1962)

— *The Letters of W.B. Yeats,* (ed.) A. Wade (London 1954)

— *W. B. Yeats — Memoirs,* (ed.) D. Donoghue (London 1972)

— *A Vision* (London 1981)